TRANSFORMING
PROJECT
MANAGEMENT

TRANSFORMING
PROJECT
MANAGEMENT

AN ESSENTIAL PARADIGM
FOR TURNING YOUR STRATEGIC
PLANNING INTO ACTION

DUANE PETERSEN, PMP, MBA, SPOC, SFC, SMC

New York Chicago San Francisco Athens London
Madrid Mexico City Milan New Delhi
Singapore Sydney Toronto

1 2 3 4 5 6 7 8 9   LCR   26 25 24 23 22 21

ISBN   978-1-264-25835-2
MHID   1-264-25835-6

e-ISBN   978-1-264-25836-9
e-MHID   1-264-25836-4

Library of Congress Cataloging-in-Publication Data
Names: Petersen, Duane, author.
Title: Transforming project management : an essential paradigm for turning
   your strategic planning into action / Duane Petersen, PMP, MBA, SPOC,
   SFC, SMC.
Description: 1 Edition. | New York City : McGraw Hill, 2021. | Includes
   bibliographical references and index.
Identifiers: LCCN 2020044370 (print) | LCCN 2020044371 (ebook) | ISBN
   9781264258352 (hardback) | ISBN 9781264258369 (ebook)
Subjects: LCSH: Strategic planning. | Project management.
Classification: LCC HD30.28 .P3738 2021 (print) | LCC HD30.28 (ebook) |
   DDC 658.4/012—dc23
LC record available at https://lccn.loc.gov/2020044370
LC ebook record available at https://lccn.loc.gov/2020044371

McGraw Hill books are available at special quantity discounts to use as premiums and sales promotions or for use in corporate training programs. To contact a representative, please visit the Contact Us pages at www.mhprofessional.com.

Contents

Foreword

As a Founder of the Project Management Institute's (PMI©) Project Management Professional (PMP®) Certification and a PMI Fellow with over 50 years in a profession, I am regularly asked to review and comment on new PM books. I have almost 300 in my personal library. These books are authored by some of the most recognized and respected names in the profession.

Occasionally a new author comes along and shifts the project management book paradigm. Duane Petersen is one of those authors. Petersen was a student of mine over a decade ago in Seattle, Washington. He was a pragmatist then, and he continues to believe that project management is *not* brain surgery!

Duane's *Transforming Project Management* is a treatise in "back to basics" that enables the reader to dispense with all the rapidly expanding jargon and the plethora of certifications. This refreshing book looks beyond the countless acronyms to illustrate the reality of what it takes to be a successful project manager in today's fast-paced, high-pressure world. Duane and I share the "Git 'er done" philosophy, and his book will provide the impetus for all project managers, no matter what type of project, to achieve success.

Petersen and I have remained connected over the years despite our separate career paths. I have focused on training (over 50,000 students in 23 countries), while he has taken the consulting path, working diligently with corporations to improve their project management capabilities. He recently completed six years in China where he assisted 7 provincial governors and 85 bankers in implementing efficient and cost-effective project management processes.

This book, like no other I have read, focuses on the importance of following the established project management process and using the proven tools and techniques to establish the foundation for creating decision support information, while executing the responsibilities of the project manager and his or her team.

In some cases, Petersen pulls concepts from industrial engineering and business techniques based on his MBA. He establishes some new methods that take project management in new directions to increase the likelihood of success. Petersen pulls back the curtain on the PM process and presents the material in an easy-to-understand format.

This book may well become the bible for any aspiring project management practitioner.

Lee R. Lambert, PMP, CEO
PMI Fellow 2009
PMI Professional Development Provider of the Year 2007
PMI Distinguished Contribution Award 1995

Foreword

The Difference Between Project Management MBA, PMP, and Pinnacle Strategist

My great-grandfather, around 1920, was a successful cattle rancher and wheat farmer. He frequently had enough money to buy new equipment and one day decided to buy an automobile as his new piece of equipment. What was that? He didn't exactly know what it was but ordered one anyway. When it arrived at the hardware store, the clerk told him he had no idea how to drive one of those contraptions, but there was a little instruction booklet my great-grandfather could read that might help. Even though my great-grandfather couldn't read, he got the basic idea of how to operate it from looking at the pictures. Besides, how hard could operating his new contraption be?

When he arrived at his ranch, he decided to park his new car in the barn. The entire ranch staff and many of his friends watched as he proudly drove his brand-new automobile into the barn.

Unfortunately, things did not go as smoothly as he thought they would. When he tried to slow down, he accidentally stepped on the gas pedal. Oops! As the car sped up, he panicked and frantically tried to remember where the brake was. He forgot that his car didn't have any brakes. In sheer desperation, he pulled back on the steering wheel and yelled, "Whoa!" That didn't help either. Instead of stopping, his car sped up and crashed through the back wall of the barn and ended up in the middle of the wheat field behind it. His only accomplishment was that he had managed to simultaneously destroy his car, wreck his barn, and humiliate himself in front of his family and friends.

Project management has a similar history, though not as well developed. When I first started in project management back in the 1980s, the only qualifications for being a project manager were that you had to have nothing else to do and no valuable skills in any other area. Really, how hard could it be? Not nearly as hard as operating a Model T with no instructions.

Then people started to realize that project management might be more complicated than previously thought. Some education might be necessary, so they invented "requirements documents and functional specifications." The idea was that each requirement identified a goal to be accomplished by the project, and each functional specification was the part of the plan that would accomplish that particular goal. Sound good? It was a much-needed improvement.

Then the business schools decided to start teaching the basic theory behind project management. Thus, we came up with the standard waterfall methodology of planning everything in extreme detail, no matter how many centuries it took and how many millions of dollars were wasted.

Next, people started to realize that project management was more of a science than previously thought and should be treated as such. So business schools started teaching this in their business school courses. But only just a bit. Next, it was realized that project management needed its own emphasis as part of an MBA program, so you could also get a good foundation in project management theory. That is the degree I have. It is a good foundation of the theory of project management, but after graduating with my MBA, I still felt a bit like my great-grandfather driving his new automobile away from the small-town hardware store with only his little booklet to rely on for guidance.

Even though my MBA with a PM focus was a big jump from the chaotic mess I experienced earlier, the PMP education and credentials I received next were another giant leap forward in organizational theory. Now I was starting to really understand more about how projects should be organized and managed.

My PMP training contained many extra parts of project management that were not included in my MBA program. I better understood how all the parts fit together: a design document, communications plan, requirements traceability matrix, risk register, and stakeholder register, along with how to make a budget, how to develop a schedule starting with good requirements, etc. This went far beyond my MBA program, which just taught basic concepts like the work breakdown structure, the network diagram, and the Gantt chart.

Even though I had made the leap from the basic MBA concepts to the more advanced PMP concepts, I still felt there must be more to come. There is still a huge leap between PMP certification and the harsh reality of trying to competently manage a large project. All this training and education, and I still had no understanding of how to accurately make a budget or schedule that I knew would work. With everything I'd learned, monitoring was still a joke.

It is not enough to have an MBA and pass the PMP exam. We need to be able to successfully manage a project on schedule and under budget with high quality while pleasing our customers by triumphing over all the potential pitfalls associated with project execution. Suddenly, driving a Model T with no instruction is beginning to sound a bit simpler.

In my never-ending effort to improve myself and become one of the best, I read this book and became the first person to take and pass the certification examination described in the book. The exam is not at all easy, as it involves essays and requires an 80 percent score to pass. Now all the confusion and frustration have evaporated. I now know precisely how to create that realistic schedule and budget and how to monitor it precisely! I've also learned much more about contracting and many other techniques to be the best project manager I can be. Yet it's much less expensive and more condensed than I could have expected.

Now project management has transformed, to use the automobile example, from that Model T with its little instruction booklet to a fully automated car that drives itself.

Robert Hughes MBA, PMP
Pinnacle Strategist

Introduction

Companies make huge mistakes every day, resulting in project failures all over the world. These mistakes stem from poor strategic planning, improper execution (project management), and/or poor leadership. Now is the time to stop the carnage and use a unique approach to discover the underlying causes of project failure, resolve those issues, and prevent future blunders.

An article in the March 2017 *Harvard Business Review* estimated the cost of IT project failure in the world at $3 trillion annually. Add all other types of project failures, and you'd have to multiply that number almost unimaginably. This book is directed at those who want and expect more from strategic planning and are tired of projects that decimate their budgets and professional reputations. Business leaders should be able to know precisely how much a major project will cost before it begins and have processes and tools to monitor how well the project is meeting benchmarks along the way. Taxpayers and politicians must be able to determine the true cost of an endeavor they have been entrusted to vote on and be able to hold subordinates accountable for cost overruns. Bankers and investors need to know precisely what an effort should cost to fund and be able to hold borrowers or company executives accountable. Adequate monitoring with meaningful metrics might even enable lenders to pull the plug on a project before it goes on life support and costs the organization a fortune.

All of this can happen when a project manager follows the methods outlined in this book. For that reason, our target market includes business leaders, project managers, concerned taxpayers, politicians, bankers, and investors as well as educators concerned with producing the next generation of business leaders. It doesn't take a rocket scientist to understand this, but the rewards to businesses and the people who can help them will be significant.

Let's examine the current situation.

The Project Management Professional (PMP) designation from the Project Management Institute (PMI) is considered the gold standard for project managers for good reason. The industry was chaotic, with each project manager attempting to invent and then reinvent the wheel with each different project. PMI brought order out of the chaos and set standards to be followed to vastly improve the industry, which are tested with the PMP examination. My point is that those standards do not go far enough to enable projects to be successful. Enabling that success is a major focus of this book.

Adherence to PMI principles is responsible for many failures because PMI bases everything on the Project Management Body of Knowledge (PMBOK), which is inadequate. It is lacking because it doesn't describe properly how to develop an adequate budget or schedule and because PMI monitoring techniques only describe how to monitor part of the budget. These are critical issues necessary to ensure project success, which immediately leads us to this question: What exactly is success?

Definition of Success
Satisfactory completion of all work necessary within the budget and schedule as agreed without requiring the addition of any time or money to make up for failure.

How can people be successful meeting this criterion if they do not understand how much money or time that project will take? Also, present monitoring techniques do not display how well the project is performing against that budget or schedule. Again, projects are launched with inadequate budgets and schedules because of lack of adequate processes, and monitoring cannot provide an adequate picture of how the project is proceeding against the budget and schedule because PMI monitoring processes do not consider all types of costs. Therefore, project managers simply don't have the tools to successfully deliver projects. So if successful delivery of a project means producing the results of the project for the budget and schedule agreed to—and your budget and schedule cannot adequately reflect what's necessary to make that happen—how is success currently possible? This is a serious flaw.

Further, status reports about how projects are progressing against their schedules and budgets are made using tools inadequate for that intended purpose because they track only part of the total cost of a project. Also, more than 80 percent of project management status reports use totally subjective stoplight colors of green, yellow, and red to indicate whether the project is proceeding on time and budget with no realistic idea of whether any of the report is accurate. This means organizations cannot understand the magnitude of a project's failure until long after the project has been completed. The organizations must then find a way to survive the ensuing mayhem and finger-pointing.

For example, one of my customers came to me after 2010, when its company had a project budget of $1.2 billion and discovered it had actually spent $3.1 billion—yet all project status reports indicated the projects were proceeding successfully on schedule and on budget. This kind of chaos is replicated throughout business and government entities daily (yes, directly due to those subjective green lights). In 2017, the *Beijing News* reported that an audit had revealed all projects in one of the provinces had failed dismally during 2012, and a team was being sent to identify the causative problems. Yes, it took five years to determine the full impact of project failures, let alone discover what might have been done to avoid them. Many organizations never even bother to look at that type of information, out of fear of what might be disclosed.

Is it any wonder why, as a neophyte project manager, I was told the final step for any project must be the bayoneting of participants? Sadly, I learned how true that statement was. The company I was with regularly terminated all but one participant at project completion, so the last person standing could aim the finger of blame in another direction.

Further, the PMP—that gold standard for project management—is awarded to candidates who successfully pass PMI's Project Manager Professional examination, yet who may have never had any actual experience managing a project; project expeditors with no decision-making authority and project coordinators with limited decision-making authority can use those experiences to sit for the exam, and if they achieve a 60 percent score on a multiple-choice examination, they pass. First, I've never experienced any examination where a 60 percent score represented anything other than failure. Second, in an examination with four multiple-choice potential responses for each question, random answers would give a score of 25 percent. For people to pass, they need to know just 35 percent of the answers, in addition to having reasonable luck.

Therefore, the examination is based on inadequate standards because of the lack of adequate processes to determine accurate budgets and schedules and monitoring. The examination requires no project management experience to take. This is combined with a passing score that anywhere else would be considered failure. This results in the designation of PMP, the gold standard for project management!

In contrast to PMI, UltiMentors, the company I founded, offers a Pinnacle Strategist designation. It certifies that the people who earn this designation have all the education and training they need to be an expert in leadership, strategic planning, and project management. Understanding this book, thoroughly, is all you need.

I also have no educational requirements other than what is provided in this book. An MBA or higher can be recommended on its own merit, and as an MBA, I will always encourage additional education. But just because academics may have a PhD behind their names does not indicate they are capable of delivering any successful strategic plans through all phases, just as no formal college degree can prevent someone from reading and fully understanding this book and the processes herein defined.

For this reason, people who understand the contents of this book can take the examination and, with an 80 percent or higher score, attain a much more significant certification than one that proves little (60 percent score required, and you still have no idea how to generate a realistic budget or schedule, as with the PMP). All that is needed for this exam is printed in this book. Also, as I will describe later, the SBOK (Scrum Body of Knowledge, which defines standards related to agile-style projects) provides significantly less than PMBOK. SBOK describes how to monitor projects as though all formulas are copied directly from PMBOK. However, PMBOK compares estimated costs with actual costs to determine how the project is progressing. With SBOK, there are no estimates because there is no advanced planning. Therefore, it's impossible to monitor estimates against actuals when there are no estimates, which ultimately sets people up to fail.

In addition, PMI requires the memorization of formulas and information such as, "You have five team members on your team. How many lines of communication do you have?" The best answer is, "Who the heck cares?" I want to hear one person tell me that understanding there were 15 instead of 14 lines of communication for a project enabled someone's project to be successful. There is no benefit in memorizing useless minutia only for the sake of academic trivia and having more questions to ask on the exam. The topics of this book are not trivial, and as noted, the exam covers only what is in the book.

I spent considerable time in China the past few years teaching my processes and discovered the desire of the people there to adopt this philosophy now. American organizations, understanding the necessity of improving their delivery, should be ready to adopt the methods described in this book to *transform project management*.

Most books on strategic planning are written at an extremely high level, and after reading them, most people will generally ask themselves why they even read the book. I don't find these books helpful precisely because they keep everything at too high a level and never broach the realistic topics related to implementing or monitoring the actual strategic ideas. This book is much more instructive and meaningful because it probes the depths of common strategic planning problems, of topics related to project management and leadership issues, in a way that will enhance strategic planning and enable it to be successful. Additionally, this book gives simple examples and walks you through specific problems with related stories that help you understand fully.

Inadequacies that this book will address, as compared with PMI, relate to budget, schedule, risk management, strategic plans, and more. You will learn how to:

- Create a budget that is much more advanced and much more realistic than current budget creation processes describe.
- Create a schedule you can depend on.
- Greatly enhance risk management.

- Break down strategic plans into a portfolio of projects and monitor the progress of projects, the portfolio, and strategic objectives correctly, without the use of worthless green, red, and yellow lights that have become the norm in this industry or the incorrect metrics defined by PMI (you will understand why they are incorrect later).
- Meld PMBOK and agile to achieve the best of both worlds while experiencing the drawbacks of neither.
- Protect yourself in contracts. Since contracting is such a critical issue, this book delves deeply into this topic so all essential aspects of contracting will assist you in being successful.

The reason there's a paucity of information regarding making strategic planning work through project management is because strategic planners, who come up with the vision for an organization, and project managers, who provide the tactical methods to realize the vision, are not the same people, tend to think differently, and rarely communicate effectively with each other.

Andre Taylor (author and speaker on business excellence), Peter Drucker (renown author and speaker on business), and Michael Porter (Harvard business professor) are three of the most influential business leaders of the past few generations. Yet none of them has written about or discussed the importance of project management in the delivery of strategic plans. All three have described "vision" constantly but apparently have no understanding of or interest in how to accomplish the vision. Dreams with no results are meaningless and potentially destructive. It seems many must rely on what I refer to as the "Samantha Stevens" method from the old *Bewitched* television show—wiggle your nose and magic happens.

Of the *Financial Times* 2010 ranking of top business schools, only the University of Iowa and Cranston School of Business in the United

Kingdom require a class in project management. The others apparently thought accomplishing strategic planning was not important.

Since 2010, the *Harvard Business Review* has mentioned project management or any project management–related topic in only a half a percent of its articles.

Again, strategic thinkers are trained to dream dreams apparently with no regard to how to accomplish them. These dreams will fail if they have no viable tactical approach—so they're essentially nightmares.

PMBOK uses only the briefest possible words to describe how project managers are to construct a work breakdown structure (WBS), make a network diagram, develop a quality budget and schedule, and so on. Most project managers, even those with PMP certification, have no clue how these things should be constructed or work together. This book resolves that situation.

This book describes a small project, then takes it the full route. We will see precisely how the WBS and network diagrams are constructed; how to generate a completely realistic budget and schedule, how to greatly enhance risk, contracting, and other issues; plus improving leadership to what is necessary for success. Then the book will further instruct how to monitor the project and all strategic planning components perfectly.

My Background

I've lectured all over the world on strategic planning and project management for decades. Trained in industrial engineering, I've taken a business process reengineering approach to bridge the gap between these disparate groups to transform strategic planning to enable success. I've consulted with 10 of the Fortune 500 companies, plus huge nonprofits and government agencies.

I began my professional career as a young MBA trained by Boeing Computer Service as an industrial engineer to streamline the workflow of a major state agency, the Washington State Department of Social and Health Services. Using my training and experience in industrial engineering, I always examined the processes to find more efficient ways of doing the work. The bane of my existence became the phrase "Because we have always done it that way." Constantly looking to improve workflow to squeeze out a little more efficiency worked its way into my consciousness, and I became passionate about it in all phases of life. There were times, however, when I definitely could have used an off switch, particularly in marriage where efficiency suggestions, especially in the kitchen, were not always welcome. My father, occasionally known for being blunt, suggested it was only consistent that I would make a career out of studying the way other people worked.

As my career began to morph into project management, business process reengineering projects became my specialty. I could utilize my skill in this area to make extremely beneficial changes in organizations while implementing software systems in manufacturing, hospitals, and so on. Soon I was offered very large implementation projects because of efficiencies the organizations would realize as a result of that implementation.

Project management is an industry defined by its failures. Each time a new public construction project is considered, the public demands information about exactly who will be responsible for the cost overruns. When projects are run perfectly, there should never be any cost overruns. The public perception, however, is quite different, and that's based on experience. People understand there are *always* cost overruns. The news is full of the Big Dig project, the Affordable Care Act disaster, and so on. As a young project manager fighting to overcome this, I decided there must be a better way to manage projects. It took only a short time to become frustrated by the entire project management profession.

I looked for guidance from the Project Management Institute but found exasperation. PMI's methods significantly improve project management and lead to consistency, which is very helpful, but not to success. I obtained my PMP and began mentoring others to pass the exam. The problems were obvious, and I was becoming too frustrated to teach it. As described previously, following PMBOK perfectly results in no successful projects unless they are seriously overfunded. How does one look students in their eyes and tell them, "Know this because PMI tells you to remember it—but do it that way and you will fail?"

I subsequently spent three amazing years in China teaching business leaders, bankers, and even provincial governors how to restructure project management and strategic planning and discovered a receptive audience eager to learn. It is my sincere hope that those in all other countries also have a similar interest.

It has often been said, "The definition of insanity is doing the same thing over and over while expecting a different result." Still, business leaders continue making the same mistakes in project management and strategic planning, causing extreme detriment to their organization in an apparent belief that this time will be different, as Figure I.1 sadly shows.

Now, it's time to stop the insanity.

This book builds upon the great foundation created by PMI and takes a business process reengineering approach for the project management industry to structure processes and ensure success. The purpose of this book is to provide a thorough understanding of how to resolve the problem of failed projects and the resulting trillions of dollars of negative impact on business and the economy. By implementing the process I introduce in the book, you'll be able to successfully improve the performance of projects. Essentially, this book will show you how to integrate project management into your strategic planning to drive organizational results.

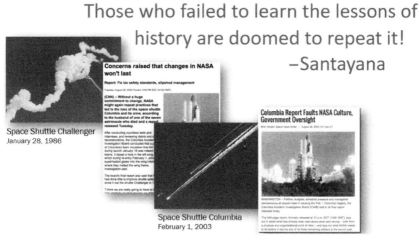

> Those who failed to learn the lessons of history are doomed to repeat it!
>
> —Santayana

FIGURE I.1 Repeating history.

I warn you all, I am opinionated because I have witnessed too much financial hardship caused by poor decisions in this profession. I provide many examples I have witnessed over the years to aid in your understanding, but in fairness to each and to avoid angering a number of former clients, I will do my best to disguise the ones with the worst decisions and practices. If it is true we should learn from our mistakes, I confess I may be unequaled in both project management and strategic planning, because I have made just about every mistake possible. My purpose is to elevate the industry in which I forged my career.

I would suggest first reading the book straight through, as the concepts will reveal new thoughts and understanding. Then I suggest reading it again carefully, examining each concept and example so you can understand exactly why everything is done as described and so you can better understand each topic. Then you are ready for the exam as well as equipped to make a career in project management.

CHAPTER ONE

Strategic Planning

Why We Need to Change Our Approach

Strategic Planning

Strategic planning is immensely important for every organization. Without it, both individual projects and the organization overall will fail.

There are wonderful examples of strategic planning done well that resulted in great financial benefit to the organization that perfected it. And there are examples of complete failures to the detriment of the organization. But mostly you will find organizations that tried hard but missed the mark. The purpose of this chapter is to examine an approach to maximize opportunities for success.

Strategic planning is the process of determining (1) where you are as an organization, (2) where you want to be as an organization, and (3) what it will take to get to where you want to be. Detailed plans to accomplish your strategic goal should result from strategic planning, giving the organization a map of how to get there.

Usually, strategic planning is done by a strategic planning team. This team is generally selected by the organization, which often hires someone from outside the company as a facilitator. Usually this group is put in charge of establishing direction for the organization. There are many methods and tools for these teams, but as you will see, there are many differences, and few organizations claim to conduct successful strategy meetings.

As long as strategic planning is thought of as an entity in and of itself, it will flounder. To be successful, project management and leadership need to be added to the mix (see Figure 1.1).

FIGURE 1.1 Successful strategic planning consists of these separate business areas.

Strategic planning is where strategic planners do their "dreaming" about where the organization is, where it should be, and how it intends to get there. However, without quality project management and effective leadership, all that strategic planning is rendered meaningless. Project management creates the plans and ensures the organization is capable of delivering but can only do so through effective leadership. Therefore, this book will examine all three as part of the same effort. If any of the three links is missing, the entire effort is wasted (see Figure 1.2).

FIGURE 1.2 The strategic planning subject area.

Choosing the Strategic Planning Team

It is critical that the best people possible be selected for the strategic planning team, because they will be responsible for defining the entire future of the organization.

Ideally, the strategic planning team should be no larger than 10 to 12 individuals in order to enable the best flow of communication. With more than 12 people, conversation tends to bog down, as several informal subgroups may form and unity begins to fracture while the meeting leader loses control of the meeting. I have witnessed strategic planning sessions where as many as 50 people were taking part. As the meetings drag on, you can see the side conversations developing. I have also seen people nodding off to sleep. So in this meeting where the entire future of an organization is being decided, people are sleeping or not paying attention. Yikes! This doesn't necessarily spell doom and disaster for the organization, but a limit of about 12 participants would resolve this.

In my experience, many strategic planning teams consist of the decision makers for the organization, sometimes some members of the board of directors, and sometimes people from geographically disbursed areas.

Senior decision makers generally are the ones selected for strategic planning efforts. The problem here is that they may have great experience understanding the organization and how it operates, but longevity may cause them to be overly invested in decisions of the past and thus incapable of being open to bold and decisive changes in a direction that could be necessary for an organization to flourish. I've heard some quoted as saying, "Because we've always done it this way and we're still around." Strategic planning should be more about thriving than surviving.

An example of how senior leaders may become overly invested happens when one of them may have been responsible for a product line that had been very successful in the past. Now an opportunity has arisen where divesting of that product line is called for. Will that senior leader be capable of making the best decision for the organization? Or will fondness for past experiences color his vision and impair him from making the best decision now?

In a competitive world, successful companies will be the agile ones, willing and able to change focus as necessary to achieve success in the changing competitive environment.

I'm certainly not discounting the value these senior leaders have to offer the organization. What I do suggest is that only two or three of the team members come from this group and that they have equal voice, not veto power. With that rule in place, they have significant representation but cannot tie the organization's hands or keep the organization living in the past by itself. This should allay some potential anger or disgruntlement from board members when they are told they will not be controlling the process.

For strategic planning to best determine direction for an organization, team members must be willing to sever any appendage necessary for the body to prosper. Senior leaders should be selected based on their ability to make the decision to cut that part of the organization that has been nearest and dearest to their hearts.

General Motors is a striking example of why this is necessary. GM had been in business for many years making Chevrolet, Buick, Oldsmobile, Cadillac, and several other models. With financial hardship looming, the company was faced with making huge, painful cuts to historic business lines. I won't say the decisions to cut Oldsmobile, Hummer, Pontiac, and Saturn were wrong. I was not in those meetings. What I will say is that, in one of my classes, when I asked students to say the first words they thought of to describe the customers for each of the brands, their answers didn't support the bulk of GM's decisions. Here are the results:

- Buick—old
- Oldsmobile—old
- Hummer—exciting
- Pontiac—fun
- Saturn—sexy
- Cadillac—rich
- Chevrolet—boring

The strategic planning group chose to hold onto old, boring, and rich brands (Buick, Cadillac, and Chevrolet). The group cut the brands referred to as sexy, fun, and exciting.

I assume that in the view of the leaders, Hummer and Saturn were new, and so they were a little risky to cut compared with the time-tested staples. In the case of Pontiac, that was the model where many concepts were tested. The leaders likely thought there was little reason for testing concepts as opposed to simply reverting to what had worked historically. I understand their point, but I disagree with it.

Not having been privy to the inner workings of GM, I have only speculation to go on regarding the makeup of the strategic planning team. When I asked the class to speculate on the possible impact of this group's decisions, the sad result suggested by one of my students was, "They just gave away the young buyers, and they are the future for the organization."

When I asked the class to speculate on the makeup of the strategic planning group that made these decisions, their responses indicated the members must have been the top leaders. The reason they stated was they looked to the past to find their future.

Never choose "yes-people" for this team. You want independent thinkers, and you want to listen to them. A strategic planning session is not about supporting a leader and forcing that person's ideas down the other participants' throats. Rather, it is about bringing in the best ideas and encouraging some potentially brash, independent, and, yes, new ideas.

In reality, yes-people are frequently selected, but not necessarily for the reason one might think. A CEO may have a few people offering consistent, strong support for executive ideas; yet many CEOs have no idea that organizational "suck-ups" have infiltrated. I will replace the term "yes-people" with "suck-ups" because that truly is what is going on. I have never been a suck-up, but I have seen so many that I certainly recognize the type. Regrettably, too many insecure leaders feel empowered by being praised and do not realize how fake it all is or how detrimental it is for the organization.

I developed my preference to identify and rid organizations of suck-ups because of a college business school class I took with a mediocre professor. There was one student who would sit in the front row and, at least twice in every lecture, raise his hand and comment, "That was amazingly insightful." The professor was totally enamored of this student, who elicited disdain plus the vomit reflex from the rest of us!

An organization might select up-and-comers for this important role. But sometimes the reason a particular person is branded as an up-and-comer is because he is a suck-up. The person in charge is impressed by this person's wisdom because he agrees with the boss.

Now that we know who not to have in strategic planning meetings, who should be on the team? As mentioned earlier, I would have up to three of the twelve be from senior management, two or three board of directors' members, and three up-and-comers (of the non-suck-up variety). Representatives from the sales, marketing, accounting, and/or finance department should make up the rest. There is one other individual that I would have, and this is someone who is almost never appointed. That person is an expert in project management.

A critical takeaway from reading this book is the importance of including a project management subject-matter expert on the team. This person is not just the common "$50 per hour," run-of-the-mill project manager. This person must be a highly skilled and knowledgeable project manager capable of understanding and performing all parts of project management. This includes understanding how to determine realistic budgets, how to break down a strategic objective into a portfolio of projects needed to fulfill that strategic objective, and so on. When you finish reading this book, you should have a very good understanding of not only what a project manager subject-matter expert is, but how to identify and support that person.

Team participants should feel their suggestions carry equal weight. Those holding more stock may have the ultimate say, but one result from a balanced approach to a strategic planning team is buy-in from the participants and from the organization as a whole. If the CEO is dominant, for example, other team members will pull back and wonder why the CEO didn't just develop the plan.

Obviously, the CEO has more authority, but for the sake of successful strategic planning, leaders need to step back from the mistake of trying to control the meeting. The same is true for board of directors' members on the team. They need to all back off from their "decision-making" role and accept more of a "meeting facilitation" role.

The facilitator of a strategic planning meeting must be granted the authority to block individuals from trying to dominate the meeting no matter who they are or what their title or role outside the strategic planning meeting may be. The best leaders are skilled at communication, and listening is one of the most important components.

Functions of a Strategic Planning Group

There are three major functions of a strategic planning group:

1. **Evaluate and assess the environment.** One common approach to this is performing a SWOT analysis (see Figure 1.3). Evaluation of the external environment for threats and opportunities as well as the internal environment for strengths and weaknesses is a crucial component of assessing the organization's situation.

FIGURE 1.3 Use SWOT to examine strengths, weaknesses, opportunities, and threats to the organization as the basis for all strategic planning.

The external environment should include an assessment of the economic and political situation as well as social and technological factors and their past, present, and likely future effects on the organization. Changing laws and social values are important to understand as exemplified by safety or regulatory changes. What about technology? Will there be opportunities for further automation? How about resources and financing?

This is when you should evaluate and compare the entity with its competitors. Evaluating where and how other organizations compare with yours will help determine your competitive strategy. Further, you might need to address ethics, which may seem old-fashioned but are critically important in this current era.

2. **Establish a baseline.** Baseline is a specific measurement at a specific point in time. For example, last month your error rate was 15 percent. That's your baseline. This month your error rate is 12 percent. This shows that your performance is improving over time versus your baseline.

   When using the baseline concept in strategic planning, you may pick a statistic such as error rate and choose a strategic objective to reduce that rate to perhaps 5 percent. Then you would follow with a plan to accomplish that.

3. **Establish a benchmark.** This is an effort to compare your organization's metrics with your competitors' and determine competitive advantages.

   Let's say your organization makes potato chips and you have hired one of your competition's leaders, who tells you that the competitor's unit cost of production is 12 percent lower than yours. To answer this with strategic planning may mean investing in new equipment and perhaps increasing production to reduce your unit cost. At this point, you could base pricing decisions on the reduced unit cost.

   Other examples of benchmarking include:
   - Your organization's research and development and how that compares with that of your competition.

- Customer satisfaction statistics.
- Profit margins.
- Product comparisons.
- Specific industry comparisons such as system uptime comparisons for software companies, sales per square foot for retailers, and so on.
- Figure of merit. This may refer to specific aspects of your products. For example, for automobiles it might include miles per gallon; for internet carriers it might refer to bandwidth.

SWOT analysis, in my experience, is generally most useful at a high level and should be taken deeply, where all levels of processes, products, resources, markets, suppliers, and so on, should be thoroughly examined to determine the strengths, weaknesses, opportunities, and threats of each.

Organizational CT Scan

Notice the term "CT scan" in the above heading. I use the term because a CT scan, a medical procedure, gives three-dimensional insight into the entire body, so any disease processes can be identified and dealt with (the hope is) before the person expires. When fully scrutinizing an organization in this manner, you also hope to discover ways to promote the long-term health of the organization.

At this point, the organization's values, vision, and mission need to be assessed. Should they stay the same or be modified? This is one of the most critical parts of strategic planning, as it sets the tone for all decisions and for buy-in. This represents the heart and soul of the organization.

Once you've established your values, vision, and mission, then you can develop a series of goals that fulfill them. These goals should be transformed into objectives. Understand, each goal and objective should be quantified. It does little good to say "more customer friendly" when "reducing customer complaints by 20 percent" is much more specific and measurable.

At this point, it's necessary to establish why goals and objectives should be measurable. In my experience, goals of "more customer friendly" result in nothing happening. Goals not fully defined will rarely be realized. If you make a goal measurable, such as "reducing customer complaints by 20 percent," thoughts, plans, and actions can be taken and people held responsible for meeting that goal. If measurements are not in place, those thoughts, plans, and actions will rarely be present and no changes or improvements may result.

When evaluating your organization's position in the marketplace, never believe that old decisions need to remain. Examine your competition, determine what and where you want to be, and make decisions and plans to facilitate that. Let's dig a little deeper on this.

In China, KFC has a huge presence and is the predominant leader in the fast-food industry. McDonald's is a distant second. Beef is available, but chicken is much more desired. McDonald's therefore made some extreme decisions to turn its second-place position around. First, McDonald's has a policy of locating its restaurants very close to existing KFC outlets. Second, McDonald's offers buckets of chicken. Third, in order to compete favorably, McDonald's now offers gourmet desserts in China. These are strategic decisions only in China because they are unnecessary in the United States and most other areas.

Always examine those companies ahead of you to find why they are more successful than you are. Examine those behind you to find if any have unique concepts that may cut into your market share. At this point, focus on where you want to be as an organization together with what it will take to get there.

When in graduate school eons ago, I was told it was nearly impossible to alter customers' impression of the quality level of an organization or its products. I continued to believe that until I watched Hyundai enter the US automobile market offering low-priced and seemingly low-end cars to the public. The world was not aware of the company's brilliant strategy. Hyundai knew few would accept its products as quality products when the company was new to manufacturing cars, and most would not consider the new brand deserving a high or even average price. Therefore, Hyundai entered the market with cars priced on the bottom end of the spectrum.

However, Hyundai's vehicles were built much better than the price tag that accompanied the cars would imply. After Hyundai had sold its cars for several years and was making a significant impact in the marketplace, consumer groups testing the cars began giving them kudos for their surprising level of quality. Hyundai then completely changed the landscape by putting its 100,000-mile, 10-year warranty in place. Now the company had market share gained from both the low price and the high warranty. Soon the notion of the company being low-end dissipated, and its cars were seen as a huge bargain (low price, high quality). Over time, this let Hyundai elevate prices to reflect the higher quality. Hyundai even successfully introduced a luxury car sporting the Hyundai moniker.

Then there is Nalley's, a great example of an organization using benchmarking. Nalley's was a major food producer located in the Pacific Northwest. While performing a SWOT analysis, it became obvious that Nalley's was having difficulty competing with its large brand-name competitors. The company discovered that Lay's offered quality potato chips for less money than Nalley's could because Lay's had a significantly lower cost per unit. Nalley's also determined that two other products it made—canned stew and canned chili—were at a cost disadvantage. Dinty Moore had a lower cost per unit for canned stew, and Hormel had a lower cost per unit for canned chili. At this point, Nalley's showed the world an example of strategic planning at its best, using the benchmarking I referred to earlier.

Nalley's made a huge investment in production equipment so it could produce three to five times more of each product than it was capable of selling under its own name. With the greatly reduced cost per unit gained from the efficiencies created by its investment, Nalley's was able to sell off its excess production to grocery stores to sell under their own store brand names. Safeway, Albertsons, and several other grocery chains began selling Nalley's excess production under their own labels for potato chips, canned stew, and canned chili.

This is a great example of strategic planning that worked. Nalley's was able to vastly increase its profit margin on the products it sold under its own label because of the reduced cost of production per unit, but also package significant quantities of products under store brand names and make a profit on all its produce sold under those other grocery brand names as well. Making this happen included marketing efforts to convince all those grocery chains to start selling these products under their own labels and to use Nalley's as their source. Because the company's cost of production became so low, it even signed a contract to produce potato chips for Lay's, the market leader in potato chips. It is rare that I use the term "brilliant" to describe a strategic planning effort, but I definitely will use that term here. One of my business professors was part of this strategic planning group, a source of pride for him, the university, and the local company—and me—since my university, Nalley's, and I were all from the Tacoma, Washington, area.

An annual or biannual reexamination can help the organization react in a timely manner to both competition and new opportunities.

Strategic Planning Components
Now it is time to design an action plan that fulfills the three goals mentioned earlier: to determine who you are, who you want to be, and what it will take (Figure 1.4). If you use the examples of Nalley's

and Hyundai, you can understand that sometimes these plans include great risk, but boldness is frequently rewarded.

FIGURE 1.4 Successful strategic planning consists of these separate business areas.

Another example of boldness occurred during the Great Depression. At that time, the world's largest retailer was Montgomery Ward, which was nearly twice the size of Sears. Montgomery Ward decided its best course of action during economic hard times was to keep most of its money outside of banks, because of the bank failures. It just held onto its money. Sears, on the other hand, became extremely aggressive, buying up stores, suppliers, and everything else imaginable to expand. It picked up all these for pennies on the dollar. As World War II began and the economy returned to normal, Sears was suddenly nearly twice the size of Montgomery Ward.

Seen through the lens of a SWOT analysis, Montgomery Ward saw an opportunity in taking its money out of banks and holding on. Sears was number two in market size and saw an opportunity to become number one and made every decision necessary to make that happen. Both firms realized their objectives. The difference? Boldness of leadership and effectiveness of strategic planning.

Now that you have developed your work plans to accomplish your strategic objectives, you must implement and monitor them as you move toward fulfilling your strategic goal.

Keep the granularity reasonable. You are evaluating the forest, not the individual trees. Reasonable granularity is necessary at this point because the strategic planning team does not have the skills to break down the work and estimate the effort, as do the project manager subject-matter experts described earlier. This is where these experts should be given free rein to make it happen, or perhaps to inform the organization about what the proper size of the effort and a reasonable budget to accomplish it might be.

In some instances, this is true, and sometimes it is not. In Nalley's case, the business leaders understood installing assembly-line food processing equipment and how to state their case to grocery chains, encouraging them to sell Nalley's products under their own labels. The effort was bold, but implementation was quite simple. Plus, the company knew how to purchase, install, and operate food-processing equipment. It had been doing that for decades.

Sears's strategic plan involved investing in any organization that was edging toward bankruptcy (as well as some that had completely expired) if the organization was a supplier or had a great store location.

The Hyundai example demonstrated how well this company understood breaking into a market. This showed great corporate strength.

This Seems Simple, Right? What Could Go Wrong?
Anything and everything could go wrong.

If you randomly approached any major organization and asked, "How does your organization's strategic planning work for you?," you would hear nothing but moans and groans. That's been my experience over decades in the United States, China, and other countries. The answer to that question and the resolution of issues related to the process are the focus of this book.

One of the primary causes of failure is a lack of understanding of what strategic planning is. In many organizations, strategic planning meetings are not meetings where long-term direction of the organization is discussed, and the meetings have nothing to do with SWOT analysis. Instead, these meetings are filled with department heads fighting for money to be given to their own departments to accomplish their pet projects. Shouting matches can and do erupt. This has become more and more frequent with the trend toward incentive-based bonuses, which of course will lead to anger and even turnover since the department heads not given their pet projects may see their opportunity for achieving their incentives disappear. Instead of determining strategic direction, the meetings become all about which department gets the resources. Misguided organizations such as these rely on return on investment to judge whether one department gets money for a project as opposed to another. Again, these companies believe this is strategic planning, but it's only a fight about where to spend money.

I watched one strategic planning meeting where it was announced, "We've not focused on Ed's department for several years, so, Ed, tell us what project you need money for." This led to two executive resignations. If strategic planning meetings exist to dole out money, they are misnamed since they are not about strategic planning. Just call them something else, like "stupid."

When an organization simply doles out money and calls it strategic planning, the organization as a whole won't buy into the plan. Each business unit not selected will feel unappreciated and left out. Leaders will see their opportunity to make larger profits diminish and view their incentive-laden contracts as being worthless. For example, if a vice president of sales has an incentive-laden contract including a huge bonus for increases in sales and believes implementing a customer relationship management system is her best way of doing that, should the organization choose to spend its money elsewhere, this person will see potentially huge financial rewards becoming greatly reduced and may make the decision to disengage from the organization.

Favoritism and nepotism are also problems when companies don't use true strategic planning. These are like dry rot in a boat. You never know exactly when the dry rot begins, but all boat owners will tell you that once it begins, you will dig out dry rot to save the boat, right up to the point you finally are forced to sell the boat so you can pass the rot to the next owner. Favoritism is the dry rot of organizations. It will eat away at everything good about the organization until it fails.

At one of my customer organizations, a department manager was involved in an affair with the CEO. It was amazing how that one department kept getting everything it wanted. The CEO had allowed himself to become compromised. When I was discussing my concern that all the other departments were jealous of the favoritism given to this one department, I was told flat out that "the CEO had an affair with that manager. Now he has to give her what she wants because the only person who doesn't know is his wife." Though office intrigue can cause many problems of this type, affairs aren't always the cause. A greater rapport with one individual or enmity with another can also cloud decision-making and spoil the entire effort.

One leader told me he hated one person in the organization more than all others and would do everything he could to get that person out, including doing everything possible to harpoon his career. ("Harpoon" was the word he used.)

Generally, most of the books and lectures I know about describe strategic planning glowingly. I agree completely! It's just in my experience, results usually are less than glowing because the efforts many organizations refer to as strategic planning simply are not.

This will also be the case if we fail to realize that the people making decisions are flawed humans trying to live their lives and thrive in a competitive arena where all is not sunshine and roses. When we choose to ignore the truth about people, strategic planning will fail.

Lack of Commitment from the Organization

One reason members of strategic planning committees are reluctant to participate is because many of these meetings are boring and full of "pie in the sky" thinking that never leads to positive results. An organization with unenthusiastic participants should address that issue straight on. If you hold these meetings just because the board of directors requires them, you're wasting your time. If you truly intend to use these meetings to establish direction and believe the assembled people are important enough to trust their assistance, then you must convince the participants that is the case.

A CEO of a banking chain once confided to me that her board required strategic planning, but she absolutely dreaded every minute of it. She described the process as being "an obtrusive waste of time." When I pressed her on this, she described meetings where the participants were organized into groups of three people each. First, she said, they were told:

- List all the problems you see with the bank.

Then they were asked to find solutions to the following questions:

- How do you see the bank solving those problems?
- In the next 10 years, what should the bank look like in a best-case scenario?
- How do you see us getting to that place?

She said the process always took a week and nothing ever changed afterward. Because nothing ever resulted from these meetings, no one ever became fully engaged. Participants hated going.

She was right. If nothing ever resulted from these meetings and they existed only because a board of directors mandated them, the entire process was a waste of time.

One would have thought the organization would be interested in the CEO's perspective. I would worry about an organization where the board of directors does not listen to the CEO—except it says so much more about the board of directors. That the board was doing what it knew was prudent is good. That nothing ever resulted indicates something else. I see this often. Many board members are retired. They know they want to direct the organization appropriately, but they just do not have the energy or commitment to see it through. My father used to be less charitable. His evaluation of this situation would have been, "Never do anything half-assed. It should be full-assed or nothing." I agree.

Not Facing Issues

As the organization performs a SWOT analysis and addresses weaknesses, sometimes what one team member sees as a strength, another may see as a weakness. Open hostility could erupt if one person feels personally attacked. To prevent this, issues that should be addressed head-on are not. Also, some organizations understand what the issue is, but internal politics make people afraid to say anything. This is especially true when the organization leader either is the issue or supports something that is not good for the organization.

That, however, is not the entire problem. Individual egos need to be checked at the door before their owners enter the room. All problems need to be identified and dealt with even when the person who may be the problem is in the room. A competent facilitator can detect conflict arising in these meetings and provide methods of reducing tension. My basic instruction is to describe what the problem is rather than who is at fault. It can be a very fine line. Point fingers at problems, not people. If a person is the problem, that should become readily evident, but the meeting must attempt to avoid open hostility, because that takes the focus from finding direction to finding fault.

I remember one meeting where a member stated, "I realize that we are always supposed to describe the problem instead of making personal observations about one of the people involved, so I will simply say, 'For some reason nothing in Bob's department is working well for reasons unknown only to Bob.'"

That being said, it is also true that if Bob is the problem, one should not say that using those words. Rather, descriptions are so much more telling, especially if they are quantified. For instance, "The sales department apparently is a weakness because:

1. Staff turnover rate is much too high. Thirty percent of employees from this department leave each year."
2. Industry average return on advertising is 3 percent. Our organization is receiving less than one-tenth of 1 percent return on advertising."
3. Our marketing literature has so much information crammed on one page that nobody is reading it. I handed our flyer to 30 people and asked what they thought. All of them responded that the document was ugly and too loaded with information for them to even examine what it says. They said they would not waste their time reading it."

Although poor Bob is the leader, these remarks are no longer personal. Rather, they describe an ineffective organization and, though Bob may be part or all of the problem, the difficulties are laid out in a way that cannot easily be ignored. Bob still may not be happy, but his happiness is not supposed to be the issue. The department is ineffective. First identify that as a weakness. Later the organization can determine the plan to resolve that weakness.

Organizational Structure

Sometimes the need to accomplish strategic planning may require changes in the current company organizational structure. When this happens, there are some key concepts that must be adhered to:

- **Examine the current organizational structure to identify necessary changes.** Is the current organizational structure meeting the needs now if the strategic planning wasn't adopted? If this is the case, perhaps examination of the current structure could lead to a "killing two birds with one stone" type of moment. As long as changes must be made, be thorough and solve the other problems at the same time. This can generate additional support and buy-in for the changes you will be establishing. This was one of my fortes as someone trained in industrial engineering. I always recommend bringing in outside expertise with no personal connections within the entity to make the structural changes in the organization. If not, make the changes—whether that means adding departments, eliminating departments, changing leaders, and so on—based upon a completely unbiased approach, if that could happen . . .
- **Build the structure around the work, not the workers.** When an organization develops around the strengths of the individuals who work there, the organization becomes convoluted and ineffective. Therefore, the structure should always be built to accommodate the work—not the people.
- **Prepare for the impact of change.** Next, take the new organizational structure and determine the best way to

prepare for the impact of the necessary change, for example by eliminating one product line and adding two new ones. Determine the best organizational structure before evaluating the leaders. Do you need to make changes? Remember that the primary objective is making the best possible decisions for the organization as a whole, which may or may not be the best decision for individuals or departments. And most importantly, prepare for pushback from individuals and departments that may feel negatively affected.

Yet changing the organizational structure can be difficult because fiefdoms develop over time. Fiefdoms. I had never really believed they could become a serious problem until I worked with an organization that reached the pinnacle of fiefdom fights. This was an organization where the vice presidents' offices were lined up in a row. I watched as one of the vice presidents took a tape measure and measured his and the other vice presidents' offices. He stormed into the CEO's office and screamed that he had four inches less space than this other vice president and he was much more important to the organization than the other vice president, and he demanded to switch offices so he would have the larger office. Four inches! They all had large, wonderful offices with water views.

Now, how are you going to modify the organization's structure to enable necessary changes when high-powered individuals truly behave like children? While childish behavior to that degree is rare, fiefdoms are real, and that makes strategists watchful and cautious.

One of the largest communication businesses believed in competition between departments and organized the business so different business units competed, even on building internal software. One organization was always picked as the winner, and the loser group was dissolved into the winning group, with the loser chief now reporting to the head of the winning department. The winner typically used humiliation and similar tools to get the loser to quit, because someday that competitive situation might repeat, and the winner did not want to face the loser again. When I asked the executives why they had such a horrible practice, they responded that competition brought out the best in people. I stopped working with this organization because I could no longer handle the horrible cloud of suspicion and anger permeating the building.

Understand, sometimes entire groups of people may need to be replaced. Yes, this can be a sad experience, but you must always be vigilant to ensure the best people are being used to accomplish the work. Square pegs can only fit round holes if we use force to reshape the peg. Use enough power, and you'll destroy the peg. It's the same with people.

Leadership

The organization is at risk because of fiefdoms, and leadership issues may compound that risk. Let's say part of your strategic plan results in selling off a long-term product line such as men's work boots to focus on buying a woman's shoe manufacturer with a line of popular women's shoes. Who is going to want to be the leader of that new line? You guessed it—the first person who will most likely want that role is the one you have just made dispensable. He will want that role, because otherwise he will risk unemployment. Now, however, you must make some hard decisions. Do you terminate the leader of the work boots product line rather than make him the leader of the new women's shoe product line? You want to show your leadership and want to show appreciation for the loyalty from this leader. The answer? You should terminate the person who led the men's shoe division if the person doesn't have the experience or excitement to make the new division of women's shoes a top producer. Is this harsh? Of course. You are tasked with making the right decisions for the organization. That means hiring the best person for the job always. The organization is more important than individuals and fiefdoms.

Other leadership issues with strategic planning, as described earlier, include providing equal voice to each strategic planning team member, encouraging everyone's input, and utilizing the results of strategic planning meetings.

Poor Governance

Experts in strategic planning refer to governance as strategically managing your relationships with external stakeholders such as suppliers and customers, as well as with your internal stakeholders who are your employees, board of directors, and management; this means managing in such a way as to maximize long-term profit and stability. The idea here is that these people are taking care of your customers, and your customers are critical to the long-term benefit of the organization. Therefore, strategic planning must encompass specific plans to effect positive changes for both. Accountability must be assigned, through management structures, to meet the needs of these defined stakeholders, as well as finding ways of accomplishing this in an ethical manner. This is a textbook definition of "accountability" and makes total sense; yet the word has become a magical elixir that, when used, causes people to stop thinking and begin nodding their heads in agreement. Regardless of whether the term is brandished or not, we hold an obligation to make certain the principle is actually applied. Always evaluate the situation and determine if the principle is actually being followed.

Frequent difficulties with concepts are related to the fact that customers, employees, and boards of directors typically have conflicting needs, and a "win" for one may result in a "loss" for another. From a governance perspective, let's return to the situation where a men's boot division needs to be replaced with a woman's shoe division. The obvious winner of this strategy will be the board of directors, because profits may jump. However, you will be changing customers and employees.

Does this mean you should avoid the strategy because of the negative effect on two of the three groups? The answer to this is no, for these reasons: First, all three groups benefit from improved financial viability of the organization. Second, customers for men's boots will be able to find other suppliers, and you will be replacing one customer group for another. Now look at the employees. Yes, some may need to be replaced, but some may just need to be retrained. Providing opportunities for employee growth and change to fit the marketplace is beneficial. There will be many more opportunities to sell women's shoes than men's work boots, which may result in greater commissions or salaries. The strategic planning perspective from that governance issue is that the organization at least consider the impact of a strategic change as it relates to each of those disparate groups of stakeholders.

Governance can also be looked at in another way. Since management structures are part of governance, we can use the term regarding roles on the strategic planning team. There can be difficulty with ill-defined roles when members of the board of directors are on the strategic planning team, as this will normally cause decision consternation among the other members. How will the board members be involved in making strategic planning decisions without denigrating or overpowering other members of the strategic planning team? Good governance of strategic planning teams would require recusal of the board members when deciding issues in which they have a personal stake, as well as necessitate constant reminders that their role includes listening and not controlling—especially if that controlling of corporate strategy may result in their own benefit at the expense of the organization as a whole.

Apparent Haphazardness

On May 15 several years ago, I was hired as a consultant by one of the largest software companies in the world to establish a major new business line. I served in this role for three weeks. At the end of the three weeks I was told, "Every June this company reevaluates all business opportunities and assigns resources for the rest of the year. The company has decided to pull funding from this project, so we are sorry, but we must let everyone go. This is your last week."

I thought, okay, the folks at the company have done their strategic planning and changed direction. Good for them. I will find something else to do.

On April 10 the next year, the same company brought me in to establish an entirely different major new business effort. On May 15 of the same year, I was told, "Every June this company reevaluates all business opportunities and assigns resources for the rest of the year. The company has decided to pull funding from this project, so we are sorry, but we must let everyone go. You have until the end of June." The words were the same, except the company gave me a little more notice.

What does this say about the company's strategic planning? I believe it tells everyone, "Take a job at your own risk because the rug can be pulled out from under you at any time." It means there is no long-term strategy. It feels like an organization totally distracted by shiny objects and just as quickly distracted by other shiny objects. An outside observer might get the idea that the entire organization makes flip decisions and that those decisions can be overturned at any moment by another flip decision. Organizations should be agile enough to adapt to new situations, but not if that flexibility is haphazard and fails to consider the consequences.

Let's compare this with the concept that governance requires making decisions to support outside stakeholders such as the customers and inside stakeholders such as the employees. Both groups will find the constant flipping from one objective to the next annoying, distracting, and counterproductive.

I never worked for that company again. Instead, I took a job with an organization that paid me less but didn't have a history of pulling the plug out from under its workers or draining the resource pool its people were swimming in. Eventually, the organization's lack of being organized damaged its reputation. Apparently, the company didn't believe that governance involves internal as well as external stakeholders.

If it happens once, it's fine. Organizations always have the right and responsibility to reexamine their direction and change course. If it happens twice in a row, it means such organizations have no long-term plan. It indicates haphazardness or, worse, randomness.

I wish the company much success. It has great personnel, but I do not believe the company's leaders are maximizing their company's capabilities for the following reasons:

- Morale suffers because everyone feels vulnerable. If you remember Maslow's hierarchy of needs theory, security sits at a basic, deep level and is necessary in our lives before any other needs can be met. Yet the entire organization sits on pins and needles waiting to see if people's livelihoods will be taken away from them with just a few weeks' notice.
- The company loses good people. Retention is difficult. If people feel insecure working for an organization that can and will axe them at any moment, the drain of good talent will begin as people look to secure their futures.
- In a SWOT analysis, this kind of governance would hardly count as a strength. Yes, the company is agile. However, when it appears you don't give a damn about your people, they will notice. Perhaps the organization is incapable of seeing the talent drain as a weakness.

- The company cannot even consider people like me a loss of talent, because out of two major opportunities, I served a little less than three months on the job. The loss reminds me of the "little boy who cried wolf" phenomenon. What are the odds that people who have lost their job more than once in this way would ever apply to that company again? Would the organization call this a loss of talent? Likely not, because that talent will simply never be available to the company again.

Organizational Culture

Organizational culture can be an almost unequaled barrier to strategic planning or any other type of success. Here are some examples:

- Someone close to me was hired to manage a major project that would have solved some major organizational problems. She was specifically ordered not to have any conversations with three people who would be major stakeholders. She was also forbidden from talking with any of their subordinates, with the threat of immediate termination should she disobey. Her project failed because, obviously, those major stakeholders' input proved to be critical to success. She was let go, and all the specific instructions by the department head, her sponsor, were reversed. She gave the department head exactly what that person wanted, but obviously the politics of the organization were poisonous.
- Another major organization I worked for had a corporate culture wherein each leader mimicked the corporate head, whose management style was to get in front of an employee and publicly scream profanity directly into the recipient's face from just inches away. I have literally seen spittle fly

from the mouth of the screaming manager and land on the face of the employee being victimized. The manager apparently believed this torment would motivate change. Instead, it motivated highly skilled people to leave the organization in droves. These screaming demonstrations were always public, to persuade all staff to hunker down and work harder. These idiots did not understand how their horrific treatment of employees caused morale to plummet, which in turn produced low productivity and high error rates and absenteeism in addition to the turnover. And it is not just an internal problem. I remember returning home from a business trip one day and taking a cab. I was asked what company I worked for. When I responded, the immediate response the cab driver gave me was, "Isn't that the company famous for treating its people like crap?" The firm was so notorious for its horrible treatment of people that even cab drivers had heard the stories.

- Ineffectiveness from poorly estimated time requirements is another leadership issue. I was once brought in by a firm to determine a method for pushing games the company developed to its commercial cell phone applications and address all the issues related to doing this. The company gave me a six-month contract to complete work that took just two weeks to accomplish. Two weeks later, I was gone. The same thing happened again when the same firm hired me for a one-year project that took just six weeks to finish. Whether the organization is simply accustomed to hiring unproductive individuals or doesn't understand the magnitude of the work required does not matter. I took a year and a half's worth of contracts that took a total of two months to complete. I was not going to charge the firm for time not worked, and I certainly wasn't going to sit around doing nothing. I hate boredom. However, I will never take a role with this organization again because it simply is too disorganized and apparently has weak management. The company needs a project management subject-matter expert to be part of the strategic planning process. What was truly the strangest part of this experience was that there was absolutely no pressure whatsoever to get the work finished in less than the time allotted. The expectations of what it would take to accomplish the work was simply ridiculous. If those extremely low expectations span the organization, then it is extremely overstaffed. People with the same work ethic as I have cannot stand to idle time away whether paid or unpaid. So I worked the short time it took to do the work, then left.

Failed Efforts

There's nothing like a history of failure to cause people in an organization to feel uncertain, unsupported, and cynical. Since project management is defined by its failures, cynicism abounds, which can doom efforts and organizations.

Once an organization begins to struggle, employees and team members bind together to save the organization and their jobs. However, when one decision after another proves ill-fated, team members begin to lose faith. When they believe the organization will fail, they may become like rats fleeing a sinking ship. That will, in and of itself, cause the organization to go down.

Now let's examine the people on a project team. This company has hired a project manager. Sadly, the company chose someone for his software development skills rather than his project management skills. Now that you have doomed the project by hiring someone who is not a project management subject-matter expert, the rats will look to save themselves because they know the project will be on a downward spiral. Would the software developer have leadership skills? Would he understand how to create a budget and a schedule that would work? Would he force everyone to build his design, or would he facilitate a team effort so a design can encompass the team's expertise? Organizations with a tradition of failure ensure future failure, because they have never understood what to do differently.

Here's a sports example. You are the New York Mets. Until 1969, you were the epitome of failure. Then you had the World Series win and immediately thereafter returned to decades of losing. Decades upon decades of finishing last in the league demoralized players, coaches, and fans. What talented free agent would want to change teams and come to a losing organization? The answer would be almost none. The Yankees are the opposite. They have a history of always winning, so many players would even take less money to play for them.

Losing begets losing. It's as simple as that.

I have been an outside consultant for decades. Organizations have brought me in for mission-critical projects. My projects have generally been successful, so I have a reputation for success. Part of the reason is that I apply the principles that I advocate in this book, but that's only part of it.

Team members do not like failure. Rarely do employees have the same confidence in their employer that they have in someone brought in from the outside. When they see someone hired from outside, eyes light up! They get excited to be involved with a project when they are confident it will succeed.

A happy team means high morale. People try harder, they make fewer errors, productivity increases, and employees are willing to forgo breaks just to get to work. All in all, if the team members believe what they are doing will succeed, the odds of success are greatly enhanced. If the team members believe the project will be a disaster, the odds of success are diminished.

Compare that to projects run by the organization's own project managers, when all those projects have failed. You get dejected team members with low morale and attendant high absenteeism, errors, low productivity, and attrition.

CHAPTER TWO

Making Sense
from Nonsense

What Is a Project Manager?

When I use the term "project manager," I'm referring to business-people, generally holding business degrees, with significant training in project management and perhaps even strategic planning. These project managers lead a group of professionals to break down all the work necessary to accomplish major business efforts, determine and monitor budgets and schedules, lead people to achieve the objectives, and monitor and report the results. Essentially, they're the people who accomplish the dreams of strategic planning.

Currently, the term "project manager" is used for almost anyone. Clerical people who manage tasks sometimes are called project managers. My experience with Microsoft has taught me that it believes a project manager is a "checklist" manager who simply marks tasks as completed or open. In some companies, order "facilitators" who track customer orders to ensure everything necessary for an order has been completed and the like are called project managers. It seems "project manager" is a popular term for people doing just about anything that cannot be easily defined. These are *not* the people I refer to in this book. I certainly don't want to denigrate these people or their work; I just want to call their work something else.

As well, the term "project" itself is often misused. The definition of a project is completion of an objective that is unique, with a definite beginning and end. This does not include regular, ongoing work. Yes, manufacturers will call order fulfillment a project; yet that work does not meet the criteria of a project because what is being done is recurring and not unique. A house being built is regular work if it's done regularly.

PMI, for some reason, never actually defines a project manager, so as long as people can show those words in a job title, they can take the PMP certification examination and, should they pass, be labeled as one of the best in the project management profession. This action denigrates those who are performing the actual job of a project manager.

The larger issue is that businesses generally don't understand what project managers are, either, so when it comes time to actually find someone to manage a major project, they seemingly have no idea whom to hire. For this reason, a business that, say, needs to develop a corporate website will promote a software developer to the role of project manager because the developer would have a great understanding of how to manage a software development project. Yet this is a major mistake. Does this new project manager understand how to work with stakeholders to determine the requirements of the project? Does she understand how to generate a successful budget or schedule for the project and monitor it successfully? How about risk? Would she utilize all team members to determine the best design for the project—or just impose her own ideas?

Yes, this person the business just hired as a project manager may have a great future as a software development manager—but that is something totally different.

This misconception is rampant across industries. I have been recruited by many companies for jobs that call for specific skill sets and technical experience managing specific types of projects—when what the companies truly needed was someone who thoroughly understood project management and how to utilize subject-matter experts for a specific industry or type of technology.

For this reason, project management has a history of failure. The best likelihood of a successful project of any kind is to hire an expert in project management, not a technical person in some desired aspect of the project.

Another point of consternation for real project managers is that many have the title but, based upon the organizational structure, those with the title never had the same level of responsibility.

- In a matrix organization, project managers are generally referred to as project coordinators because they have a small amount of responsibility and can make some decisions, but not many. They are not in a leadership situation, as they share leadership with the functional manager.
- In a functional organization, project managers are generally referred to as project expeditors. A project expeditor has no authority to make any decisions, as that authority is given to the functional manager.

Yet project coordinators and expeditors do apply for job positions as project managers, and organizations generally are so thrilled when they see project management experience on a similar project in a different organization that they hire this applicant believing the person possesses the requisite skill sets and knowledge to accomplish what the organizations need. As described earlier, without the skills and experience based upon the organizational type, they simply are not seasoned project managers. Yet, these people's experience allows them to sit for the PMP certification exam, and with knowing only 35 percent of the answers in addition to reasonable luck—ta-da!—you have a PMP who knows little about project management and who has little to no realistic project management experience. Organizations leap to hire these project management experts with "just the right experience" and are shocked when everything promptly goes to hell in a hand basket!

Those who read and understand the depth of this book will prove to be a top-of-the-line project manager. They will be true project manager subject-matter experts, wherein junior project managers, coordinators, and expeditors are excluded. I hope business leaders of all types understand this point, because their businesses will benefit greatly if they do.

What Is the Difference Between Strategic Planning and Project Management?

The biggest disconnect between strategic planning and project management is that the thinkers and the doers are different personality types, each having little to no understanding of or patience for the other. Not only that, but project managers are almost never included in strategic planning. The real reason for this is that strategic planners want the ideas unencumbered by practicality. The other reason is that project management, for some strange reason—perhaps because of its reputation for failure—has never been considered a leadership, or C-level, skill set. Regrettably, these are the reasons strategic planning generally doesn't work.

Here's why it is important. The strategic planning team is generally tasked with coming up with work plans to become what the organization wants to become. The team also comes up with budgets because projects take resources, and as we all know, resources are limited. The difficulty is that the people determining budgets have little understanding about what achieving the plans will take in terms of time and money.

From a slightly different perspective, let's say we have completed a SWOT analysis, and while coming up with potential projects to enhance the product for customers and to make life better for our employees (since both these types of efforts result from governance issues defined earlier), we must find a means of comparing these alternatives since there are normally insufficient resources to do everything. Therefore, the organization decides to use an ROI (return on investment) approach to determine the economic value of each of the alternatives. How do you determine the value or even the cost of those alternatives? This book describes this process thoroughly, but strategic planners have little to no insight into these processes, and so, in the end, the organization guesses. This process describes the way nearly all organizations determine which projects to accept in strategic planning scenarios, and because there is no project management subject-matter expert to bring realism into the scenario, the result, truly, is that nobody knows.

Let's take this scenario one level deeper. You decide to go to the bank to borrow money to accomplish the project you have selected. When the banker finishes laughing at your pathetic attempts to explain how you determined the required funding levels, how do you obtain the loan? Here is how. You pay much higher rates because of the risk you pose to the bank. This might have been resolved had you been able to justify your cost figures thoroughly and thoughtfully.

The banks making these loans are the real organizations at risk. One bank I am very familiar with recently loaned a huge housing construction project many millions of dollars. The bank was given documentation on what the project would cost and what the amazing return on investment was planned. The bank jumped at the chance to loan the money. The developers, of course, overestimated how much people would pay for the homes and how rapidly they would be able to sell the units, because those numbers came from salespeople who are always optimistic about what can be sold. It was the cost figures, however, that nearly put the bank out of business. The bank was forced to continually add more funds while praying it was not just throwing good money after bad. Yet if it didn't keep loaning more money, the development would have gone out of business, which could have ruined the bank. This situation is repeated in almost every bank in the world. For this reason, my software product that enforces all the tenets of this book is under consideration to be adopted by Chinese banks. They want to be able to determine precisely how much something will cost so they aren't making a bad loan. For this, they will offer organizations using the software a significant interest rate reduction to entice them to use the product.

Antonio Nieto-Rodriguez, former chairman of PMI, is a true spokesperson for PMI, and his book *The Focused Organization* has had a large impact in the project management community. I cite him in important ways, because he truly understands the shortcomings in the industry, though his conclusions are absolutely shocking, as you will see. In his book, he asked the question, "Why do executives neither understand project management nor feel it is overly important?" His conclusions are that the executives:

1. Lack a basic understanding of how strategic projects relate to overall strategy
2. Do very little to increase project management competencies
3. Fail to implement formal project selection processes
4. Lack the means to monitor strategic projects

Before going on, I must state that although I agree with all four, the biggest reason the executives don't understand project management or feel it's important is due to the lack of respect that project management gets, as described below, plus the historical failures of project management, which I will be addressing later in this book.

We addressed the first issue in the Introduction.

As stated before, project management is the fulfillment of strategic planning. Leadership is what guides the entire process. All parts must be in place and working together to enable strategic planning to work. Why major universities and business writers can't see this is a constant mystery to me.

Rather than modify the technical issues related to improving project management, Nieto-Rodriguez believes strategic planning works best when—drum roll please—organizations focus efforts on fewer initiatives. While I do agree if you do less you may fail less, my intent is to modify project management to actually fulfill strategic planning. Doing more or doing less should not matter if you do it right and well!

Yes, Antonio Nieto-Rodriguez is a major thought leader of PMI who simply accepts that projects fail, and so the best a company can do is to rely on it as little as possible. I disagree completely. If you manage projects correctly, they will not fail.

This book bridges that gap!

Antonio Nieto-Rodriguez's First Point—Lack of a Basic Understanding of How Strategic Projects Relate to Overall Strategy

Project managers and strategic planners need to work together so strategic thoughts can lead to tactical methods for implementation.

As previously described, there are many methods for determining a strategic plan. It's not the purpose of this book to evaluate alternative methods for determining strategic direction. Rather, this book is intended solely to evaluate processes to ensure the success of whatever strategic direction is selected.

In Figure 2.1, you can see how the strategic vision should result in a strategic plan, which in turn will be achieved using the tactical methods.

Any company can have a big vision and strategic plans,
but it requires clearly defined tactical methods to succeed.

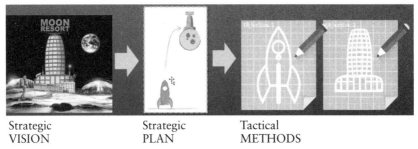

Strategic   Strategic   Tactical
VISION   PLAN   METHODS

FIGURE **2.1** Vision to plan to objective to delivery.

Figure 2.2 is a great way of showing how individual projects relate to the strategic objective. Not only can you see how they physically relate; you can see how the production of each is related to the whole.

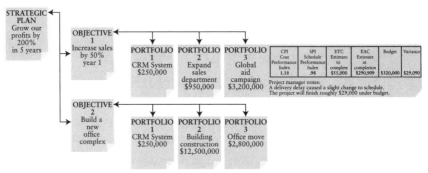

FIGURE **2.2** Strategic performance monitoring.

Example of Strategic Planning

An example of strategic planning would be to decide that an organization will increase sales by 50 percent each year. With people in the company working together, how does an organization accomplish that?

Strategic planners and a project manager subject-matter expert working together could break down this strategic objective into a portfolio of projects, such as:

- Implement a new customer relationship management (CRM) system.
- Reorganize sales, including channels of distribution.
- Launch a global advertising campaign.

After proceeding through the proper way to determine a budget as described later in this book and monitoring it correctly, we could be seeing a dashboard something like the one shown in Figure 2.3. In the figure, the positive results are highlighted in light gray and the negative news is highlighted in dark gray. Each project of the portfolio should be "rolled up" so one can see its impact on the strategic

	CRM	Reorganize	Advertisting	Objective
Budget	$1,425,220	$3,634,215	$18,231,550	$23,190,985
Earned Value	1,140,176	1,853,450	2,364,631	5,358,357
Actual Cost	950,000	2,400,000	1,900,000	5,250,000
% Complete	80	51	12.9	23.5
% Budget Spent	66.7	66	9.6	22.6
Work to Budget	13.3	–15	3.3	0.9
CPI	1.2	0.77	1.2	1.02
EAC	1,187,683	4,719,759	15,192,958	22,736,260
Variance	237,537	–1,085,544	3,038,592	454,725
ETC	237,683	2,319,759	16,331,550	17,486,260

FIGURE 2.3 Proper monitoring example.

objective. This will seriously deliver on Antonio Nieto-Rodriguez's fourth point: the lack of effective monitoring tools.

The figure shows what is known about the strategic objective to *increase sales by 50 percent*:

- The strategic objective is 23.5 percent complete.
- Since 0.9 percent more work has been completed than budget spent, this means the organization has spent slightly less than expected to reach this point.
- The CPI is the cost performance index. If it is above 1.0, the project is performing better than anticipated. If lower, there are difficulties. In this example, the CPI is 1.02, which is quite reasonable.
- The EAC (estimate at completion) adjusts the budget based upon the current productivity (CPI). In this case, the strategic objective will cost $454,725 less than expected to be completed—as noted in the variance.
- The ETC is the estimate to complete. To achieve the strategic objective, $17,486,260 will be needed.
- Attention should be paid to the Reorganize Sales Channels Project, as it seems to be having difficulties.

Figure 2.4 presents another example of an appropriate monitoring chart.

Antonio Nieto-Rodriguez's Third Point—Fail to Implement Formal Project Selection Processes

Obviously, an ROI basis for project selection is much more positive, fair, and beneficial to the organization than the "money dole-out" approach described in the previous chapter.

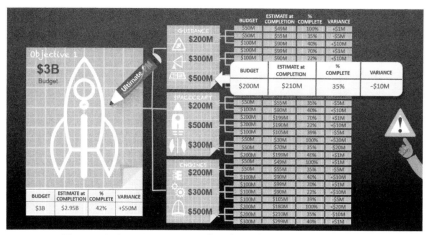

FIGURE 2.4 Using system developed metrics, a detailed reporting of performance data to the level of activity is immediately available to stakeholders.

Well, that's how it's supposed to happen. The issue? How does the organization determine the cost and the return to plug into ROI formulas? These are usually rough order of magnitude (ROM) estimates determined by the sponsor. The real issue is how that sponsor determined the estimates. Are the estimates from strategic planners with no concept of what's necessary to realize their dreams? If no tactical experts or project manager subject-matter experts are present in the room for strategic planning meetings, then numbers coming from strategists are meaningless at best. Or are these estimates from sponsors wanting their pet project accepted over all others? According to PMBOK (the Product Management Body of Knowledge), ROM estimates at best are considered no more than plus or minus 50 percent accurate. Up to now, project managers could not give realistically accurate input into the cost, but they can break down what would be involved in making a project successful, so they can at least reduce the likelihood of crazy, out-of-line estimates. Therefore, ask yourself: Are the estimates tainted in any way?

This situation has become a boon for the unscrupulous. In these circumstances, winners of the strategic planning extravaganza (sponsors getting their pet projects selected) will be the ones who exaggerate the most. In one situation, the VP of sales negotiated a great contract for himself: his bonus was determined by increases in sales. For this reason, he wanted a CRM system implemented. Since his organization selected between strategic objective alternatives based on projected ROI, he decided to vastly inflate projected revenues and understate projected costs. Yes, the technique he chose is also known as "lying." He would get his personal cash cow approved, and the project manager would be blamed for the overall failure.

However, instead of reaping the benefits of his treachery, the company lost so much money due to the resulting mayhem that it went out of business and was forced to sell out to a company a fraction of its size. Even so, the project manager was still blamed. The smaller company retained the unscrupulous vice president, and he led the lessons-learned effort to determine where to point the finger of blame.

ROM estimates are totally insufficient as selection information. Never should numbers be accepted from those standing to benefit personally or in any other way from the effort. The best solution would be to bite the bullet. Pay to locate and bring on a project management subject-matter expert to develop a budget for each strategic objective under consideration. This will increase the cost of deciding which projects to implement, but the effort will pay for itself many times over by enabling a full understanding of the potential ROI and assist the organization to prosper at the highest level possible through investing in its strategy.

As you will understand from Chapter 3, "Developing a Rock-Solid Budget," even hiring the best project managers out there will result in budgets that have no relationship to what will really occur.

Closely examine what PMBOK says about selecting between alternative strategic objectives. The guidelines describe using mathematical methods like net present value (NPV) or internal rate of return (IRR) to evaluate the time value of cash flow for each alternative—with the highest number NPV or IRR selected. Consider the origin of the numbers for those estimates. We've already discussed why you shouldn't have people financially benefiting from their pet project being selected, nor should you accept the numbers from strategic planners without project managers being part of the equation, but these are only parts of the problem. Think of these highly scientific mathematical methods being utilized to evaluate numbers based upon guesses. That is the state of the industry. When asked where the numbers for return, cost, or time came from, the answer usually refers to a wild guess—or to be a bit more colorful, a scientific wildass guess, or SWAG.

Again, these SWAGs came from which people? Did those people understand what the requirements were? Of course not. Were they from a department head who wanted her project selected? Likely. If you asked for a detailed breakdown of the work necessary to accomplish the effort, could that person deliver? Probably not.

Through a thorough analysis with project managers and strategists working together, strategic objectives will be based upon somewhat more solid numbers.

However, should you utilize the budget development process presented in this book, these will be rock-solid budget numbers. Mysteriously, when this is done, NPV and IRR numbers suddenly become totally reliable.

Projects Have Been Selected—Now What?

A large part of this book is dedicated to resolving Antonio Nieto-Rodriguez's second point—doing so by increasing project management competencies.

My first very large project occurred many years ago and consisted of selecting and implementing complete financial and clinical systems in a 12-hospital group before there was a Project Management Institute, at least that anyone knew about. Luckily, as a young MBA specializing in operations management and with my training in industrial engineering, there were a lot of positives to begin with. I had a good idea of what I wanted to do and how I was going to do it, which was a must. Had I not been able to persuade the organization that I understood the best approach to performing this project, the organization would have never given me the chance, because a 25-year-old rarely gets this type of opportunity. Therefore, I presented the group with a detailed plan of attack specifying how I was going to perform the project. My plan provided so much more detail than anyone else's that the group was convinced I could perform on the contract adequately. Apparently presenting a well-thought-out plan was considered safer than an evolving, seat-of-the-pants operation. Of course, it is easier to convince an organization that we will be successful when there is a complete plan of attack. The competing organizations were the large accounting firms that essentially, without tailoring any presentation specifically for this organization, took their traditional approach, which included:

- Stating that anyone who doesn't hire them is crazy.
- Showing the amazing résumés of partners who would likely never even hear about the project, let alone be available to it, but certainly would have many hundreds of dollars per hour applied to the bill.
- Never providing the organization with a bottom line of what their costs would be. Yes, total flexibility for everyone except the customer.

Since this was prior to PMI becoming known, this meant having to track everything on paper and coming up with my own processes to accomplish the work. Though it proved to be a successful effort, it was a total seat-of-the-pants operation. I had to decide on my own what people I needed for team members, how to obtain requirements from stakeholders, and absolutely everything else. Then, of course, I needed to train all the team members to use my, shall we refer to it as "well-established processes"? Convincing my team, the organization, and other stakeholders that these developed-on-the-fly processes were time proven and vital for a successful project was absolutely necessary to accomplish the project. Utilizing Microsoft Project for MS-DOS proved to be more complicated than just using graphic paper.

Consider for a moment the pressure on my shoulders as a man with no experience performing this kind of work armed only with a good education. I needed to be successful. So I read as much as I could from as many "experts" as I could find. There obviously was nothing like Google back then to instantly find answers to any questions. Yet, as stated earlier, one of the best ways of having a successful project is by having the organization believe it is going to be successful. I maintained an air of confidence, which the team maintained until the end. And, yes, I am glad I was also trained as an actor so nobody would notice my knees shaking.

Presently there is PMI, which offers a basis of understanding that can get project managers to almost 50 percent of where they need to be to be successful.

Sadly, although PMI is the organization attempting to elevate the project management industry to a set of standards, most project managers have not had the education or training to determine what is necessary. Therefore, project management is the same seat-of-the-pants operation for them as what I faced on that first project of mine. I at least had the education and, I suppose, the chutzpa to pull it off. The fact that organizations continue to promote software developers, engineers, and all sorts of other people good in their professions into project management roles with little to no training in project management simply exacerbates the problem.

Even when an organization hires a project manager for this role and that person has studied all the PMI books and precepts, that project manager would still be unsuccessful, because PMI standards fall far short of what is necessary to be successful. This book examines each less-than-fulfilled standard.

The Crux of the Issue

The most perplexing issue to drive the point home is that the definition of a successful project is delivering the agreed-upon scope for the agreed-upon budget and schedule. PMI does not provide adequate information to create either successfully. If a book written by a leader of PMI maintains that the easiest way to fail less is simply to do less, that is the heart of the problem!

What PMI Does Very Well

PMI describes the beginning of a project very well, even though it only touches on the strategic planning elements. It describes how the project manager, through an interview with the sponsor, creates a project charter. This is a great beginning. A project charter has two purposes:

1. To authorize the project
2. To give authority to the project manager

Figure 2.5 is a great example of a project charter.

Some of you may remember paper job applications. These would normally include a half-inch square of open space, capable of holding approximately 10 letters, in which applicants were directed to

Date: ___/___/___

Project name and description:

| |
| |

Project manager assigned: _____

Project Manager Authority

Yes	No	
		Spend time as necessary to define and plan the project.
		Provide a budget and schedule for approval based upon defining the work.
		Authorize purchases as necessary to fulfill the project. If not, has the authority to spend up to $ _____.
		Recruit and terminate staff as necessary.
		Commit funds to mitigate risk if the EMV of the risk is higher than the cost.
		Make decisions as necessary to accomplish the project.

Business case:

| |
| |

Resources pre-assigned:

Name	Role

(continued on next page)

FIGURE 2.5 Sample project charter.

Stakeholders Known:

1	
2	
3	
4	
5	
6	
7	

Requirements Known:

1	
2	
3	
4	
5	
6	
7	

Product Description/Deliverables:

1	
2	
3	
4	
5	
6	
7	

FIGURE 2.5 Sample project charter (*continued*).

Measurable Project Objectives:

1	
2	
3	
4	
5	
6	
7	

Project Approval Requirements:

1	
2	
3	
4	
5	
6	
7	

Preliminary Risk:

		1 to 5
1		
2		
3		
4		
5		
6		

Project Manager Signature: _____

Sponsor Signature: _____

FIGURE 2.5 Sample project charter (*continued*).

describe their role in each position they have held, one space for each position. If their role could be defined in 10 letters, they never did anything worth describing. However, that same format is used on most project charter forms. These documents say to describe project manager authority in a space that generally has room for 10 letters. Apparently, nobody wants to get specific, or it is simply too much of a bother to have to think about it.

Good project managers should want to know precisely what authority they have prior to accepting the project. I would never accept a project manager role in an organization where I would be subject to micromanagement from someone less experienced or less knowledgeable than I am. Besides, using cagey word selection could enable this document to provide more authority than the sponsor intended. The example of the project charter in Figure 2.5 defines specific issues critical to understand for managing the project. If project managers want more responsibility defined, they should do so.

In most project charters I have reviewed, that little section describing project manager authority has been left empty. Apparently, project managers either want to assume ultimate authority to do whatever they feel necessary or have no clue about what they should be doing, or they are simply so happy they got the job that they do not care. Generally, I encounter the "no clue" or "don't care" situations most often.

There is no budget nor schedule in the project charter, as there is no idea at this point what work is necessary to be completed. Requirements must be gathered, evaluated, accepted, and estimated before this is possible. If the customer requires the budget and schedule to be included in the charter and demands you manage the project for the apparently random number you are shown, you should note those as constraints and state, "After requirements gathering is complete and the entire project estimated, the true budget and schedule will be determined and evaluated against the constraint. A go or no-go decision can be made at that time, or the scope can be reduced to meet the constraint."

Sometimes the organization truly does have a limited amount of money available for the project. By developing the budget adequately, a project manager subject-matter expert should be able to say, "I cannot give you all the requirements as presented by the stakeholders, but this is what I can give you for that amount." This presents a far superior alternative than simply trying to manage the project with no true understanding of the cost and just crossing your fingers that the project ends before the money runs out.

The best use of these "constraints" currently may be for the accountants to show how far off the mark the project was after it fails. Yes, this is also where the old definition of a boss comes in handy. "A boss is someone with the authority to delegate blame."

I have used this "After requirements gathering" statement many times when organizations really wanted me to manage a project for the amount they allocated. This may make sense from a limited resources perspective. After I break down exactly what the entire budget and schedule should be, I produce a document that fully describes budget components, so the organizations can see all the details. I then proceed to give them options for which deliverables could be cut to deliver the product for the budget and schedule they want. The advantage of this method is that scope can be negotiated and the organizations can make the decision about what they are capable and desirous of paying. However, it is known, the organizations will have a budget that is realistic, as well as a scope agreed to that can be produced for the budget they wish to provide. Doesn't this seem more palatable than just waiting until the end of the project and having to explain the failure?

One of the largest healthcare organizations in the United States prohibits project charters by culture. The reason is because management refuses to be "tied down." This gives management the flexibility to completely change the project on the fly. For PMs, this presents no end of frustration. Some features would be outside the business case, but who cares? Management can decide willy-nilly to add them back in. Planning is endlessly ongoing because nothing is ever locked in. Budgets and schedules are meaningless since they will keep changing. In one of the projects I managed for the organization, a specific requirement that would add about $180,000 to the project was rejected by the organization. Later it was accepted only to be rejected again. This in-and-out process happened eight times! Managing this project became so frustrating, I'm convinced part of my baldness came from pulling my hair out from requirements flowing in and out of scope. I have made it clear to that organization that I will never manage a project without a project charter and would not have taken the project I did manage for the organization had I known it was going to refuse to use one. To drive the point home, PMI now states, emphatically, that anyone who manages a project without a project charter is unethical! Good for PMI! Yet what does this say about an organization that demands you proceed without a charter?

One last issue regarding project charters. A corresponding project closure form should be used for every project, whether completed or shelved, that compares the outcome with what was stated in the project charter. This document should address the following issues:

- Business case—did the project meet the business case or not? Explain.
- Project deliverables—delivered? If not, why not?
- Measurable project deliverables—which were met or unmet and why?
- Under what circumstances was the project ended?

The project closure form should go to the sponsor and original customer and be archived with Lessons Learned.

Success Never Defined Is Never Achieved

There's a box in the project charter for project approval requirements. Most organizations never define what constitutes success until well after the projects are completed. Let that sentence absorb for a few seconds. The reason? Not defining success at the outset allows for creative interpretations after the fact. Over the years I have witnessed many bizarre and, yes, creative interpretations by twisting words and truth to prove that a project was successful when it was a disaster! These include such gems as:

- "We delivered what we promised even though we had to add to the budget and schedule quite a number of times."
- "The customer may have been a little upset with what we delivered. However, they paid so everything is fine."
- "Our projects are always successful. If we need more time or money to finish the project on time and on budget, we just generate change orders until we have the project completed on time and on budget." This quote was provided by a military contractor who maintained that his company always made a profit because the government always accepted the company's change requests. Change requests are supposed to be for scope changes only where budget and schedule can be increased to accommodate additional work. I asked if his company ever purposefully underestimated how much a project would cost so it could win contracts, then "change-request" its way to profit. The response was, "Of course, we're not stupid." My response was, "No, just unethical." This also proves that government procurement practices need serious improvement. As you will see in a later chapter, government is not the worst in this arena.

All the above represent failed projects. I prefer using the contractual definition of success. From a contract perspective, as stated several times to this point, a project is successful when it is delivered as defined in the contract (scope) for the price and schedule agreed upon. Anything else would be considered breach of contract. Do what you agreed to do for the price and time agreed upon. If you fall short in your performance, you fail. No finagling of terms or truth is necessary.

Why does this concept seem so foreign?

Perhaps the answer lies in reality. If we have no idea regarding how long something will take or how much it will cost, then project management is an effort in futility anyway. If an effort in futility, just do what you want and who cares—besides investors, boards of directors, customers, sponsors, and those types of people? Now add to this the reality that most budgets and schedules are being determined prior to the requirements being known, and there lies . . . ah yes, insanity. Enormous sums of money and resources are committed to gigantic efforts with little understanding of anything. Sadly, this is the current state of strategic planning and project management. There should be little difficulty at this point understanding why project management is known for its failures, right?

One last issue relating to project budgets. I have witnessed many project managers who have what they consider to be a very successful tool to get enough money for their project. It's called inflating budgets, and it is considered unethical by PMI. When I told this to a class I was teaching one time, a student told me, "But it is necessary. Whatever budget I give to the owner of my company, he will cut it by 15 percent and give that to me for a budget. Therefore, I have to always inflate my budgets by 15 percent to make up for what he will cut." My response was that her boss recognized she was always inflating the budget by 15 percent and perhaps was taking steps to counter hers. I suggested she just talk with him about it and agree that she would not inflate by 15 percent if he wouldn't cut by 15 percent. She looked at me like I must have come from Mars. She couldn't imagine such a thing. I still think that is strange.

For those of you who believe you can generate a successful budget and schedule, please continue reading and see if you were right. Challenge yourself!

The next few chapters are intended to reduce the insanity.

Gathering Requirements and Other Information

The process the project manager goes through to gather requirements and information is typically haphazard at best. If the project manager seems unorganized, stakeholders and team members lose confidence. The impacts of lost confidence include a much greater likelihood of the project ending early, low morale, low productivity, increased errors, and everything else that is just "wrong." If the project manager can maintain an air of confidence by knowing exactly what to do and doing it, the odds of the entire project being successful are monumentally increased. It's always been a curiosity to me that acting confidently can help you be successful even if you have no clue what you are doing, but it's true.

Most importantly, many projects fail because a crucial stakeholder may have been overlooked and requirements missed. These are the reasons for the emphasis on process for this chapter.

Most good project managers know they need to get requirements and information on risk from stakeholders as the stakeholders become identified. But if the project managers continually visit and revisit stakeholders looking for information, the stakeholders get perturbed, then angry, then lose all confidence that the PM can do the job. Soon the project is on the ropes. All these problems stem from the project managers not having an organized approach to information gathering.

To streamline requirements gathering, I suggest simply completing a requirements traceability matrix (Figure 2.6), a stakeholder register (Figure 2.7), and a risk register (Figure 2.8) based upon information garnered from the sponsor while developing the project charter. Then show the documents to each stakeholder identified by the sponsor and ask:

- What requirements are missing?
- Which stakeholders are missing?
- What risks are missing?

Then repeat this process with new stakeholders as they are identified by other stakeholders. Please note, before you show these documents to each new stakeholder, you will want to revise them to include all the additional information you've garnered. This organizes quickly and reduces multiple contacts with stakeholders, which otherwise would waste time and aggravate them. Each additional stakeholder will be treated the same way as you ask the three questions and complete the documents. If you can categorize stakeholders into groups such as customers, users, employees, and so on, and then meet with them in groups, the meeting notes should result in notations to each of these documents.

Now you have all you need from stakeholders and can begin to plan your project.

Please know that the forms shown in Figures 2.6, 2.7, and 2.8 also make a great communication device. If you are utilizing SharePoint or a similar document management tool, these documents should be readily available for stakeholders to examine. When stakeholders can see if their requirement was accepted and when it is scheduled or why refused, morale is good. When a team member has a question

Project Title

Requirement	Business Objectives	Relevant Information	Owner	Work Package	Status	Scheduled Completion	If Not Accepted— Reason

FIGURE 2.6 Requirement traceability matrix.

Project Title

Name	Title	Contact Information	Expectations	Influence	Role	Responsibility	Other Information

FIGURE 2.7 Stakeholder register.

Risk	Description	Identified By	Impact High/Low?

FIGURE 2.8 Risk register.

related to a specific work package, the member can see who specified the requirement and check directly with that person for additional information. Plus, everyone's contact information is readily available, so those working on the requirement can resolve questions easily with the person impacted.

Don't Dump PMBOK's Most Important Tool

The work breakdown structure (WBS) is by far the most important tool PMs have for planning projects. This is where first the preliminary team and then the actual team collaborate on how to organize and perform the work necessary to accomplish the project. The work is broken down into smaller and smaller refinements until all the work and processes to accomplish the goal are known and can be estimated. At that point, the cost in time and money is estimated for each step, which then becomes the basis for the budget and schedule.

From my experience, less that 10 percent of all projects are begun with a WBS. Instead, planning is done completely on a Gantt chart. Skipping the WBS is akin to saying, "Who cares what work we have to do, how long it will take, or how much it will cost? We will begin just by scheduling the work." To not utilize a work breakdown structure is beyond ridiculous! How could the very basis of the budget and schedule not be important enough to use? Any organization that allows a project manager to manage a project without a work breakdown structure deserves the disaster that will then ensue.

I guarantee that I will never hire a project manager who does not have much experience creating a WBS and that I would fire any working for me that I see not using one for traditional project management. This is the most important tool of project management. To begin the project with a Gantt chart is lazy and completely detrimental to the project and the organization needing the work to be completed.

Yet this is so pervasive! During an interview for a position leading the project management department in one Fortune 500 organization, the interviewers asked me to show them one of my project plans. I asked, "Do you mean a Gantt chart?" Their response was, "Yes—your project plan."

I asked if they also wanted to see one of my WBSs and network diagrams and how they flowed into the Gantt chart. I was told, "We don't want to see all the crap, just the result." I then had to tell them that if they believed a Gantt chart was a project plan, I was decidedly not the person they wanted nor would support! At the end of the day, it's your project's schedule.

Without a comprehensive approach to determining what work to do, one will never be organized or understand costs or schedules, and the project has little chance to be successful.

After team members have collaborated by constructing a WBS and have worked together to estimate the time and expense of each piece of work, a network diagram is used to organize the work, along with a Gantt chart to display the schedule.

Since most project managers I speak with tell me they have looked at all the PMI materials but still cannot figure out how to construct a WBS, I will do so now. The example project is extremely small, but the same process should be performed regardless of the size of the project.

The example will continue to be utilized as we go through a full example of creation and refinement through each of the topics in this book. This will demonstrate exactly how to put each part of the budget together and how each project management topic will affect the project.

The project is to replace an existing deck on a house. Milestones (the highest level of the WBS) should include:

- Designing the new deck
- Removing the existing deck

- Obtaining the materials
- Constructing the infrastructure
- Constructing the surface of the new deck
- Adding the rails

As we break the milestones into work packages and activities, those could be the following:

- Designing the new deck
  - Determine size.
  - Make decision.
  - Perform all measurements necessary.
  - Determine type of deck to build.
    - Design the infrastructure.
    - Design the surface.
    - Design the railing.
  - Determine materials to be used.
- Removing the existing deck
  - Tear down the existing deck.
    - Destroy surface.
    - Destroy rails.
    - Destroy infrastructure.
    - Remove.
  - Load truck.
  - Transport old deck materials to the dump.
- Obtaining the materials
  - Compute the quantity of each part necessary to fulfill the design.
  - Procure.
    - Determine contract type for purchase.
    - Produce bid document.
    - Select potential vendors.

- Submit to three vendors.
- Receive and evaluate bids.
- Complete procurement.
- Constructing
  - Add the posts.
    - Dig the postholes.
    - Add cement to the holes.
    - Set the posts.
    - Secure the attachments to the house.
  - Construct the bracings.
  - Construct the surface.
- Add the rails.
  - Top.
  - Add the bracings.
  - Finish.
    - Prepare.
    - Stain.
    - Clean up.

Figure 2.9 shows what this would like graphically. You can easily see how the project gets broken down into smaller and smaller parts. The WBS numbering system enables you to see precisely where in the project each work level falls. The whole numbers, 1, 2, 3, and 4, are the milestones. The numbers at the next level, with one decimal point, are the work packages, which may or may not be further broken down. Those with two decimal points are all activities. Remember, the work gets broken down into small enough parts that each can be estimated.

When we get to the budget section, we add hours plus dollars. Team members will be estimating the cost. For this example, we will assume that each of the team members will cost $50 per hour just to make it easy.

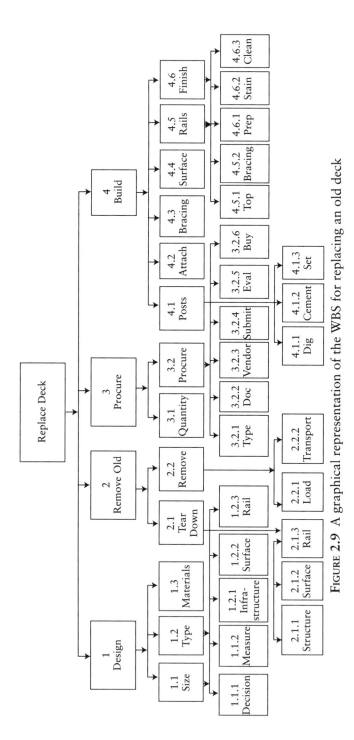

FIGURE 2.9 A graphical representation of the WBS for replacing an old deck

We will drive this small project through budget and schedule, so everyone can see exactly how these components are produced.

Figure 2.10 presents a small computer-generated example of a WBS. My objective is to force all project managers to use this tool fully and completely, as it is the most important tool for a project to be successful. As you can see in the figure, a WBS can relate to an entire strategic objective.

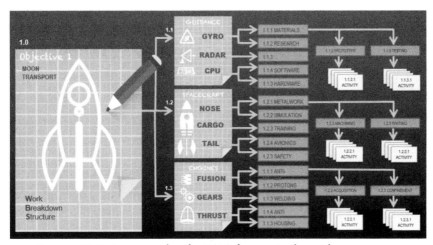

FIGURE 2.10   An example of a WBS for a missile guidance system.

If you follow the process defined by PMI, your project will likely fail for other reasons. But we are making progress! If you keep eliminating issues that cause projects to fail, you get closer to projects that do not fail. At least that is the hope!

Example of a Network Diagram

The network diagram is completed by taking time estimates from the WBS and determining the order in which activities must be completed before a different activity can begin, which activities can be scheduled simultaneously, and so forth. Figure 2.11 provides an example. The numbers in the small boxes identify how long a par-

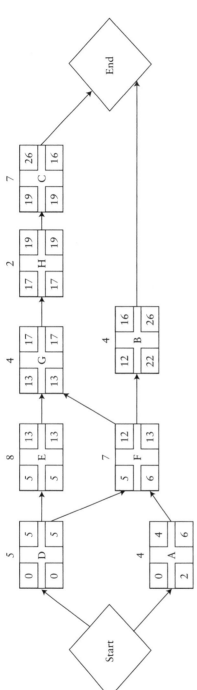

FIGURE 2.11 Network diagram for the deck corresponding to the deck replacement project described in Figure 2.9.

ticular activity can be delayed and still have the project finish on time (slack).

The longest path through the network diagram is the critical path. The reason it's called that is because the critical path defines how long the project will take to complete. Any delay to an activity on that path will extend the project unless extraordinary measures are taken to modify time expended.

For the over 98 percent of project managers who do not use a network diagram, how do you determine what the slack is on each activity? How do you determine how long the project will take if you do not understand what the critical path is? When I ask project managers why they don't use this diagram, the answer is nearly always the same: they don't know how to. It's really quite simple, but PMI, in its Project Management Body of Knowledge, fails to adequately define it. Again, it's not my purpose to teach the basics of project management. It is, however, the purpose of this book to point out why project managers are failing and what organizations should be able to expect of the PMs working for them. For me, it's critical enough that when I interview prospective project managers for hiring purposes, I ask them to describe how to make a network diagram and use it. If they don't use it or know how to use it, I will consider them only for a junior position.

A bit later, I will take our deck construction project above as an example to build a budget, including how to estimate time and money requirements. Then we will make a network diagram and have it flow into a Gantt chart. Here I will simply describe what PMBOK gets wrong regarding network diagrams.

- PMBOK tells project managers they should focus their attention on the critical path since any delay on that path delays the project. I believe all paths need to be monitored, and the software I designed emphasizes that. Here is my reasoning: Let's say that a 30-day delay happened in receiving servers for the server farm necessary for the software you're building to manage and that the slack for the project is only 5 days. Even though the delay is not on the critical path and thus you may not have noticed it, your project is now expected to take an additional 25 days. So the project manager who assures the business that its project is on time and on budget has no idea not only that the project will be 25 days late, but also that the team to will have to be paid for an additional 25 days. This means you blew both your budget and schedule. Congratulations! You followed PMBOK and failed your project.

- I explain in the reason why SPI (schedule performance index) as defined by PMBOK is meaningless. PMBOK states that if the SPI is less than 1.0, you're ahead of schedule, and if you're over 1.0, your project is behind schedule. However, this is only a slight indication since without the network diagram (over 98 percent of the time), the project manager has no idea which activities are on the critical path. Your people can be accomplishing much on a noncritical path–related activity and yet ignore those on the critical path. Since the critical path defines how long the project will take, the project manager just delayed the project—even though the metric indicates the project is on time or ahead of schedule. This is yet another example of following PMBOK not being successful, but in fairness, PMBOK does describe project managers as unethical if they don't use a network diagram.

CHAPTER THREE

Developing a Rock-Solid Budget

Insanity Begins at the Top

It has been my experience that top managers determine project budgets and schedules nearly 80 percent of the time. Mission-critical projects happen with no more effort to determine a budget than executives making a guess.

The correct time for management to provide ROM (rough order of magnitude) estimates is during strategic planning when strategic objective concepts are floated and high-level costs and benefits are evaluated to determine the future direction of the organization. Even at that point, you've seen precisely why companies shouldn't use ROM estimates. The problems with these figures being used for the project include:

- ROM estimates are considered by PMBOK (the Product Management Body of Knowledge) to be no more than 50 percent accurate

- There is no agreed-on scope, as no requirements have been identified or evaluated.
- The work has not been broken down or evaluated

A New and Better Method for Determining a Budget

Overview

Meaningless budgets and nonsense monitoring are a constant frustration for all C-level leaders. Most people understand that budgets for projects and strategic objectives are meaningless because they've experienced their ineffectiveness for years. The state of the industry may as well be called "Pick a number." Status reports are typically those subjective colors of green, yellow, and red, or metrics as defined by PMBOK that will, if generated perfectly according to PMBOK's directions, monitor perhaps 40 percent of the costs correctly. Understand, PMBOK was totally correct in its elimination of subjective colors. It used metrics to replace them. And those metrics would be perfect if they just included all project-related costs.

Our objective is different. From this chapter you will gain an understanding of precisely how to build an accurate budget and monitor it effectively. The aim is that, at any point, management will be able to look at a dashboard that's similar to the ones at the beginning of this book, for example, one that combines a portfolio of projects relating to the strategic objective, and say something like: "We have completed 31 percent of the work and spent 35 percent of the budget. At the current pace, we expect to complete the effort $72,000 over budget."

PMI describes how a budget is created by taking time-related costs determined by the work breakdown structure (WBS) and then adding the risk reserve from the expected monetary value (EMV) of risk plus estimated procurements. You can see this performed in the deck replacement project example as we continue to construct it. If performed perfectly, this might get within 40 percent of the true cost. That's not close enough.

Figure 3.1 shows a typical diagram of budget components. As you can see, the actual work is the major portion of the budget, but typically over a third of the budget involves other costs, such as:

1. Nonproductive and nonworked time.
2. Staff meetings.
3. Initiation and planning. These two categories relate to using the team to determine requirements as well as the project manager's cost. Though the project manager may not have a budget for these costs, they are direct costs to the project. Accountants will charge them to your project whether you agree or not.
4. Project manager's time. Yes, the project manager expense is a direct cost.
5. Time value of risk. Please note, this is not the expected monetary value of risk defined below. The time value of risk is a proprietary term from my company. It's based upon the concept that many risk elements are risks of delay. For example, if there is a 50 percent likelihood of a server farm being delivered 30 days late and your team costs you $10,000 daily, then $0.5 \times 30 \times 10,000$ equals a time value of risk (the expected time value, or ETV) of $150,000.
6. Monetary value of risk. This is the component of risk understood by PMI. An example of EMV would be a 20 percent chance that rain in significant quantity at the wrong time would damage a building's foundation and necessitate the reconstruction of the foundation, which may cost

$100,000, which equals 0.2 × 100,000, or $50,000 of the expected monetary value of risk.

7. Recruitment and training.

8. Incentives.

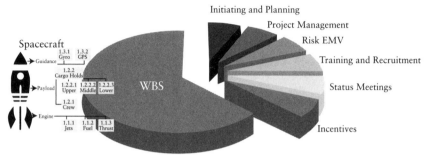

Work breakdown structure (WBS) includes labor, expenses, work-related meetings, procurements, quality efforts, etc.

FIGURE 3.1 Actual costs necessary for inclusion in project budgets.

Figure 3.2 shows the PMBOK-defined budget. These are the only project-related costs PMI defines. Yet there's so much more.

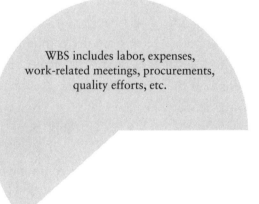

FIGURE 3.2 Traditional project management (PMBOK) method for developing project budgets.

Our Budgets Are Constructed Much Differently, Though They Begin Alike

PMI adequately defines how to generate the budget for the work related to performing the project. It involves taking the WBS and estimating each activity defined or the work package if it cannot be further broken down. Estimating means determining the amount of time necessary and converting that into dollars, as well as adding costs related to each, such as expenses or procurements. After each is rolled up to the work package level, each work package is then rolled up to the milestone level.

We begin with the WBS we described earlier, in Chapter 2, as part of our deck replacement project. Remember that we broke the WBS into four major milestones. We then dissected each into the work packages necessary to deliver the milestone, and then we broke the work packages down into activities to deliver the work packages. The next step is to enter the time and cost.

Figure 3.3 shows what the WBS chart looks like when hours and costs have been added to each activity and to the work packages if no further breakdown was needed. When there are activities under a work package, the hours and costs from the related activities are accumulated into the appropriate work package. Work packages are rolled up into the related milestone with hours converted into dollars, assuming a flat $50 per hour for each of them. According to PMBOK, we would have a budget of $18,985 plus any possible EMV of risk— to be addressed in Chapter 10. We would schedule this assuming 317 hours according to the WBS.

Estimating

First, perhaps we should discuss just how those estimates were created. Here are some basic methods:

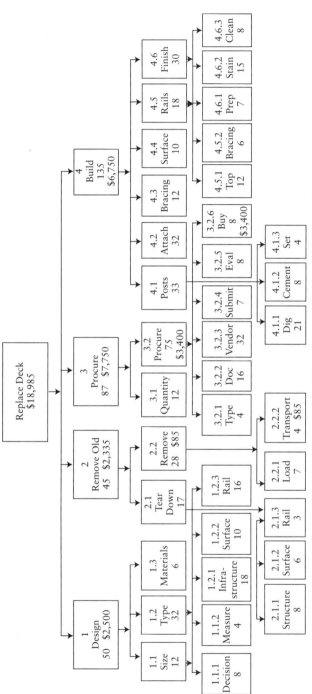

FIGURE 3.3 A graphical representation of the WBS for replacing an old deck with quantities and costs.

- **Historical information.** This method makes use of what was learned from the different projects. After each project has been completed, a document called Lessons Learned and other documents should be maintained. As projects are being completed, actual times should be noted so the organization, if ever doing a similar project in the future, will have a historical record to use for guidance. This history should be able to increase the accuracy of future estimates.

- **We need to address the issue of who will be breaking down the work and estimating costs.** PMI asserts that the team of people who will be doing the work should be the ones doing the estimating, but that rarely happens. The reason is that the budget will generally be determined well before you hire or select the people you need to do the work. Breaking the work down also helps you understand which skill sets and how many of each will be needed, so how can the ones doing the work be the same people who are breaking down the work and estimating? The question then becomes, who will help you break down the work and do the estimates?

Usually, when creating the project charter at the beginning of a project, there is, as you saw in Figure 2.5 in Chapter 2, a section called "Resources Preassigned." This is where you should be recruiting and obtaining subject-matter experts who have successful experience doing this kind of project. These people are the ones who should be breaking down the work and doing the estimating.

- **The Delphi technique.** This technique refers to asking an outside expert. The term "Delphi" comes from ancient Greece. Delphi was the place where all the leaders and brilliant philosophers such as Aristotle, Plato, and Socrates would go to seek guidance from the high priestess in Delphi, often referred to as the Oracle.

A modern example of the Delphi technique would be a cellular company that wants to replace its current cell towers with towers that use the latest technology. One suggestion might be that you ask a cell company in another country (so not a competitor) that may have already implemented the newer type of tower so you can receive pointers or talk with a consultant with expertise in that area.

A downside to having subject-matter experts estimate how long work is going to take is that these people tend to be smarter and more talented than your average, run-of-the-mill workers. This means they may give a number that represents how long it would take them to do the work, but maybe not the average worker. Therefore, you must remind them to estimate as if they were average. This type of estimating is referred to as one-point estimating, which is normally all one will need.

- **Three-point estimating.** For this method, the organization has three people estimating durations. To get an estimate that is as accurate as possible, the three people use the following formula, which attempts to "normalize" their estimates:

$$D = \frac{P + 4(M) + O}{6}$$

where D is the duration, P is the pessimistic estimate, M is the estimate in the middle, and O is the optimistic estimate.

This formula attempts to put unusual estimates into perspective. For example, three estimates may come in as 50,

51, and 70. Obviously one estimate is quite different from the other two. The three-point estimating technique considers the outlier but does not give it equal consideration. I'd ask the person making the high estimate what she saw differently. She may have discovered a risk or an issue the others didn't consider. I'd address that issue prior to utilizing the results of the three-point estimating technique. In other words, resolve seemingly out-of-line estimates prior to accepting the estimates.

- **Monte Carlo simulation.** In this method, thousands of simulations are done to determine the likelihood that the project will complete on any given day or that any particular activity will be on the critical path, and the method also makes any number of other bizarre claims. However, remember how these estimates are generated— they are just guesses. They don't consider such issues as capacity planning. I find it fascinating that so much money and effort supports this kind of logic. The tools are good, but they don't accomplish what they proclaim because the benefits are greatly overblown. Humans make estimates, but they don't have all the necessary information. So they are only giving a top-of-the-head evaluation.

Capacity Planning

If you believe that the number 317 in our WBS example represents the amount of time for which you will be paying, you will be sorely disappointed. People following PMBOK have no idea that the budget just created is not even close to what it will eventually cost. The largest culprit is capacity planning. Capacity planning, in a project management situation, means team member work capabilities. Budgets and schedules must allow for nonproductive time and time not actually worked.

Nonproductive Time

A study by Chris Gaetano published on June 7, 2017, in the *Trusted Professional*, a newspaper of the New York State Society of Certified Public Accountants, showed that just 39 percent of available work time is spent in productive work. We will adjust that to 50 percent because 11 percent of the eliminated time was for meaningful meetings. We account for meetings in a different way, as you will see later. Taking smoking breaks, going to the restroom, talking about football, texting, reading email, scanning the internet, responding to emails, taking and placing personal phone calls—this time is real and must be accounted for. A 2011 study by Price Coopers stated that 40 percent of work time was not productive, and so we must take into consideration all the distractions.

When you ask people how long a task will take in the WBS, they will probably give a number representing heads-down working (as opposed to heads-up dreaming, aptly captured in Figure 3.4). They will not include wasted time—but this time must be accounted for because it is real. You must pay for 50 percent of the time when nothing is produced. This concept has long been understood by those in the field of industrial engineering, but not by management or project management. Therefore, we adjust working hours by doubling the time estimated.

FIGURE 3.4 What nonworked and nonproductive time can look like.

Nonworked Time

How many times have you heard the excuse, "It was not my fault. Thanksgiving and Christmas caused many people to leave, and we just didn't have the manpower to work at full speed." Vacations, sick time, and holidays and other nonworked time must be accounted for. It's simple to do. Assume a 5-day workweek, which equals 260 working days per year. Each team member uses 10 vacation and sick days each year, plus 10 holidays, plus an additional 14 days for the average time spent in unrelated meetings and training. That number is now 34 days. Therefore, 34 of 260 days translates to a loss of 13 percent of work time. If those employees are legally required to have two 15-minute breaks daily, that means 7.5 hours are available for working in a day—a 6.25 percent reduction. Add the 6.25 percent for breaks to the 13 percent for holidays and vacations and other unrelated activities—and nearly 20 percent of the time you pay for is not even worked.

We've demonstrated that the impact of nonproductive time and time not actually worked is equal to nearly 70 percent of all available time (50 percent nonproductive, 20 percent not worked), so team members are effectively working productively only 30 percent of the time. Many bosses try to intimidate workers into working harder by browbeating. However, as PMI correctly maintains, that simply reduces morale and reduces productivity while increasing errors, making matters even worse.

To adequately reflect the impact of nonworked and nonproductive time, estimates for each work package should be divided by 0.3, which reveals the true time that work package will take.

The only way to reduce this 70 percent wastage is with incentives. Failure to include this 70 percent in your budget results in vastly unrealistic budgets and unachievable schedules. If you want to take full advantage of this, incorporate incentives like those described in the next chapter. It discusses the best way you can overcome this problem.

Figure 3.5 provides the best possible example to give you a visual understanding of the impact of capacity planning on your budget.

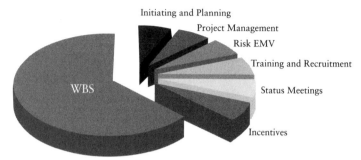

FIGURE 3.5 Reiteration of necessary costs to determine the budget.

I'm reminded of being in the room with a representative from the vice premier of China and a group of Chinese provincial governors as I described capacity planning. One of the governors became quite indignant. He stated: "We are Chinese. We work harder than people in other countries."

My response was to ask him if he ever watched construction projects in China. He responded, "Of course."

I continued, "When two or three workers are hoisting tools to higher levels of the construction project, what are all the other workers doing? They're watching, right?"

Further, nearly all construction projects in China have high walls around the construction site. The fun speculation I heard from many when I asked the purpose of building the wall around the site was "to hide the workers when they are not working."

At this point, the vice governor of Hubei Province, who had been the project manager of the Three Gorges Dam project (the largest dam in the world), spoke up and said, "He [meaning me] is right! We only believe that our people work harder than people in other countries, but people are about the same wherever they are." At that point the other governors nodded in agreement.

The governor who made the statement about the Chinese working harder was certainly correct in one aspect. The Chinese culture has people working longer hours per week generally. I specifically was referring to work as performed in the United States. The percentage of nonproductive time may need to be adjusted in other cultures. Perhaps dividing by 0.3 will be modified a little in other countries, but the concept remains the same.

If you are a manager, you may dream of the day your workers spend 100 percent of their time working at maximum efficiency. However, people are not perfect. Some work harder than others. If you have smokers on your team, smoking breaks generally reduce productivity. If people smoke while working and not during a break, their overall productivity is greatly reduced. I've done industrial engineering time studies on smokers and found them to be working at about 20 percent of normal pace while smoking.

My cousin was a machinist who worked for a major airplane manufacturer. He was dedicated to the firm and went to work on a day he had the stomach flu because he knew how important his role was to keep his team from falling behind schedule. However, his company was implementing a productivity-enhancement process with a monitor that tracked and measured the time each person entered and left the bathroom. When my cousin got called into his boss's office and questioned about why he spent so much time in the restroom, he quit. While his company believed its monitoring would improve productivity, the company so offended a good worker that it lost him.

People are not perfect, and some days are better than others. Just account for the productivity issues or use incentives as described later in this book. Understanding this gives estimates more complexity.

Now we return to the deck project. As you remember, we included 317 hours to do the work, with a budget of $18,985. Dividing the 317 required hours by 0.3 to account for nonworked and nonproductive time, we now have to pay for 1,057 hours of work. The cost is $52,850 for labor, plus materials and expenses of $3,485, for a total project budget of $56,335. This figure will be much closer to reality than the smaller number that doesn't reflect capacity planning. Without capacity planning, we would have set the project budget at $18,985—a number that would have given the project no chance for success.

Loading and unloading will work better with more than one person, and the project will take 1,057 hours, so we will assume that 4 people will be doing the job. You will see why this is important to the budget and the schedule later. Divide 1,057 hours by 40 hours per week to get 26.5 person-weeks. Divide this by 4 workers, and this gives us 6.7 weeks to complete the project.

Generally, when I teach a class how to do this, at least one student assumes that just one person will do all the work. If one project takes 400 hours, then one person could do it in 10 workweeks. In reality, you can decide how fast the work needs to be done and change the number of people assigned accordingly. Do understand the two side issues to this, however. First, as more people are assigned to the task, more coordination between them is necessary, which will cause slightly longer project durations. Second, some tasks don't go faster when you throw more people at them. Nine women cannot give birth to a baby in one month.

As we discuss additional budget issues, we will continue to bring in our deck project, so we can see the impact on the total.

Accounting for Meetings

During my lectures, I frequently ask project managers if they account for meetings, and if so, how do they do it. Only one or two per lecture say they have ever accounted for meetings. The ones who have say they consider the time as overhead. I disagree.

Overhead refers to expenses like electricity or janitorial services. You have to pay those bills, but they aren't directly related to the project. If meetings are not related to the project, then why have them? Conduct no meetings that are not related to the project. Additionally, if the project manager has no control over the meeting, that speaks volumes about the lack of control the project manager has in other areas.

If meetings are not included in your budget, the project has severe difficulties. Accountants will not be able to subtract meeting time from the personnel costs allocated to your project just because you forgot to include the meetings. The cost of meetings will be charged to the project whether the project manager considers them related or not.

To account for meetings, take the average hourly team member cost (for example, $50) and multiply that by the average number of team members expected to attend meetings (let's say 30), multiplied by the average meeting duration in hours per week expected (in our example, 2), multiplied by the number of weeks in the critical path (50). For this example, the budget for meetings would be $150,000.

These hours need to be included in the schedule. In our previous example, we expect 3,000 meeting hours. If you don't account for this in the budget and schedule, you harm your chances for success.

Controlling Meetings

Meetings are necessary for a plethora of reasons. Wasted time in meetings is a huge problem. Every minute spent in a meeting is a minute the team is not working on the activities defined in the WBS. Therefore, the project manager should focus on how to make each meeting as short and meaningful as possible.

There are three "gets" for meetings: get in, get what you need, then get out. Minimize nonproductive time and get people back to work fast.

How can you better manage meetings?

- Always have an agenda, provide the agenda early, and stick to it.

- Do not allow time-wasting discussions about unrelated topics.
- Begin on time, and don't repeat information for late arrivals, even if they're important people.
- If someone wants to continue talking about an unrelated topic, just table that discussion for after the meeting and proceed with your agenda. Refuse to allow one individual to hurt everyone's productivity.
- If you can avoid meetings or adopt a scrum meeting approach (15 minutes daily), do.
- Always end meetings on time or early—never late.
- Be creative. Because meeting rooms were scarce on a government project early in my career; the weekly status meeting had to be held on Friday at 1 p.m. The team members almost fought to keep the meetings going so they could go home after the meeting without returning to their desks to work for the rest of the day. Essentially, they wanted the meeting to give them an entire afternoon break from work. It was extremely difficult to persuade them to finish the meeting and return to their desks for work. I gained the upper hand by removing the chairs from the conference room before the meeting began. Everyone except the project manager (me) had to stand. Meetings suddenly became very efficient: 20 minutes and back to work. I wasn't going to let others ruin my odds for a successful meeting without trying something desperate.
- Because meeting efficiency is important to productivity, consider adopting an Intel approach: The door is locked five minutes after the meeting begins. The door is unlocked when the meeting concludes. It is never opened in the middle of a meeting to allow anyone in, no matter the person's position in the organization.

- Personnel evaluations note each time someone accepted a meeting and didn't attend, including when the person did not get there before the door was locked. If the organizer begins the meeting or ends a meeting late or behavior is disruptive, the organizer is penalized. These evaluations result in consequences that range from bonus reduction all the way to potential job loss.
- Don't allow meetings ever to run late, because that sets a bad precedent for the next meeting.

Businesses can become much more efficient with enforced meeting management. I've heard that Intel morale is generally high, because people don't enjoy having their time wasted when some other group infringes on their time by being late.

I go one step beyond Intel for my meetings. I have a cell phone box at the door into which people need to place their phones, and I tell people that if they are caught instant-messaging on a laptop, they will have a letter of reprimand placed in their personnel file directly following the meeting. To maintain efficient meetings, we need attendees to apply their full attention.

Some businesses have ridiculous concepts regarding meetings. One gigantic customer in the Northwest demands a team meeting daily if the project is having difficulty meeting its target so the company can stay on top of the issue. It's even worse when the project lags behind or is over cost. In those instances, two daily meetings are required. For some reason the company simply cannot conceive that the meetings are taking the team out of productive work and jeopardizing the projects. Every time I notice people in high management positions making decisions like these, I remember the Peter Principle: people are promoted from areas of competency to a level where they're incompetent.

Failure to manage meetings effectively results in project failure. That's why Intel takes meetings seriously.

A Better Scenario
Each time a meeting approaches, the project manager should consider whether there's any way to avoid the meeting altogether. If you only need to get status reports each week, perhaps just walking through the worker site and checking with workers for a minute or two is enough. Then write up your notes and avoid the meeting altogether. Now productivity continues to hum, and you have all you need.

Meanwhile, back to our deck rebuilding project. As you remember, our original time of 317 hours and budget of $18,985 was expanded to 1,057 hours and $52,850.

Because there are only four people working on this project, I imagine that we will need one meeting per week, so they are ready to hit the ground running. They might be able to get by with one 30-minute meeting per week and an additional 2 hours work time per week over the 9.7 weeks. Said another way, this is an additional 13.4 hours to be added to the project. This means the 1,057 required hours is now 1,070 hours and the cost has added $650 more, for a total of $53,500.

Initiating and Planning
The project officially begins when the project charter is signed. However, this does not mean that costs begin after the charter is signed. The business will charge all preliminary costs: interviewing stakeholders, determining requirements, planning, and so on. What about the project manager's time during that period? The bean counters will apply these costs to the project whether the project manager remembered to account for them or not. Besides, these costs truly should be allocated to the project since they are directly related. The

good news? When all planning is complete and the project is ready to begin its execution phase, you should know what your preliminary team and project management time has cost to this point. Remember to add that number to the budget.

On our deck project, we will assume it took the team of 4 people 1 week to determine the work breakdown structure and estimate all the costs. With 4 people meeting 40 hours per week, we get an additional 160 hours. This balloons the budget by an additional $8,000 to $61,500.

Project Manager Expenses

Only a few project managers include their own fees in the budget. Just like accounting for meetings, the project manager's budget figure should be that person's weekly cost, multiplied by the number of weeks in the critical path, plus one to three weeks for closing the project.

Project managers often have trouble estimating their own costs because they have no idea of the critical path, and that's because they are part of the 98 percent of all project managers who do not use a network diagram. Work is difficult without the right tools.

This concept arose with a particularly painful educational experience for me. Early in my career, I was an outside consultant for a government entity. I calculated and tracked the budget. Then I lost my job because I spent all the project money early. The reason? The customer accounted for the money it was paying me, and it had to fly me in each week and pay for my hotels. I had not included any of that in the budget. I decided this would happen only once. If project managers learn from their mistakes, that makes me an expert—I've made many.

Back to our deck rebuilding project. It's a small project that likely requires only a half-time project manager oversight. Our six-week duration has expanded to seven weeks, plus an additional week of planning, so we will need a half-time project manager for eight weeks. If we are paying the project manager $60 per hour, we must add an additional $9,600 to the budget, bringing the grand total up to $71,100.

Expected Time Value of Risk

Traditional project management does a fine job of defining how to determine the ETV of risk. But it fails to consider the time value of risk. In the following example, a delay has both a monetary impact and time impact. If the team must be paid when delays occur, the impact on the project could be huge. Just as the budget is impacted, the network diagram and the Gantt chart are as well.

In my experience, Lessons Learned in this situation would usually describe a delay that project managers couldn't anticipate or plan for. Baloney! In a software implementation project, there will always be a risk of delays associated with receiving servers and getting them set up and working. Further, there will always be a risk of a server failing to boot up because it was damaged in shipping or any number of other problems. In construction, many problems may cause a risk of delay. The cabinets delivered were not as ordered or wanted, for instance, or they simply wouldn't fit. Plan for delays. Figure 3.6 presents one small example.

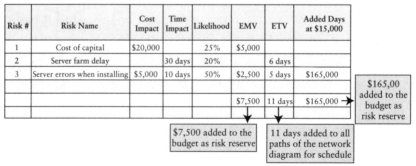

Risk #	Risk Name	Cost Impact	Time Impact	Likelihood	EMV	ETV	Added Days at $15,000
1	Cost of capital	$20,000		25%	$5,000		
2	Server farm delay		30 days	20%		6 days	
3	Server errors when installing	$5,000	10 days	50%	$2,500	5 days	$165,000
					$7,500	11 days	$165,000

$165,00 added to the budget as risk reserve

$7,500 added to the budget as risk reserve

11 days added to all paths of the network diagram for schedule

FIGURE 3.6 Revised example of quantitative risk analysis.

Adding the time and cost value of delays to the expected time value of risk is a critical improvement in how risk is addressed. Remember, projects fail if they go over time as well as over budget. Also, if you need to keep your team longer, that decidedly will impact your budget.

To return to our deck replacing project, we have evaluated risk and determined the cost and time impact, likelihood, EMV, ETV, and ETV daily cost, as shown in Figure 3.7. Now you can see both how and why the project has been impacted minimally, in this case, because of risk. Again, the $340 EMV of risk is traditionally the only part of risk in the WBS budget. Further, as you can see, it's only a fraction of what the true cost of risk will be. Therefore, we must always consider the ETV of risk.

The described budget for the project has now expanded from $18,985 to $19,325. Are you beginning to see why traditional budgets have little chance of success?

The amount our little deck replacement project will now cost has risen from $71,100 to $79,920 (adding both the EMV and ETV).

Risk	Risk Name	Cost Impact	Time Impact	Likelihood	EMV	ETV	ETV Daily Cost
1	Raining when digging holes, pouring cement, setting posts, or finishing		3 days	0.5		1.5 days	$2,400
2	Assumption that no inspection was necessary proves not to be true		10 days	0.25		2.5 days	$4,000
3	Inspection demands structural changes	$2,400	8 days	0.1	240	1 day	$1,600
4	Materials not of satisfactory quality	$1,000	3 days	0.1	100	0.3 day	$480
					340		$8,480

FIGURE 3.7 Sample deck replacement project quantitative risk analysis.

We will assume there was no training or recruitment necessary for this project, which means the final, tradition-based budget figure would be $19,325, instead of our $79,920. Which number do you feel is more appropriate?

Now think at a higher level. Imagine that you are a state legislator considering how to vote on a major new project. You have been told that the requested budget figure has been calculated based on the highest-quality levels from traditional project management. Knowing what you know now, would you confidently vote for this project, realizing the budget will likely be significantly under the amount presented and the project undercapitalized?

Now put yourself in a banker's shoes. A business customer presents a budget for a project it wants you to fund. The customer says, "This project budget has been developed using traditional project management methods." Would you loan the customer the money?

Training and Recruitment

The best way to plan for training and recruiting costs is first to understand the individual skills necessary and skill levels (whether for an expert, someone capable of performing the work, or a novice) necessary to perform project tasks and then to estimate the quantity needed for each. Figures 3.8 and 3.9 are examples of histograms used for this purpose.

The first histogram (Figure 3.8) would be a simple list of skills necessary for the project. If you are lucky enough to get a good preliminary team assigned to help you define and plan the project, these subject-matter experts should also assist in developing resource histograms.

#	Skill
1	
2	
3	
4	
5	
6	
7	
8	
9	
10	
11	
12	
13	
14	
15	
16	
17	
18	
19	
20	

FIGURE 3.8 Definition of skills required.

The second histogram (Figure 3.9) would show the skills on top, with each rated by the number of workers needed with these skills and the required skill level: expert, capable, or novice. Generally, should an organization use cross-company resource histograms, it will list every skill conceivable on the skills matrix list. The workers would individually list the skills they have and rate themselves on each. The skill levels of available team members are then evaluated against each skill required, with the resulting gaps requiring recruitment or training. Over time and many projects, project managers should adjust the ratings up and down based upon performance.

Team Member Skill Requirements by Skill

	1	2	3	4	5	6	7	8	9	10	11	12	13	14	15	16	17	18	19	20
Quantity of Above Ratings for Each																				
E																				
C																				
N																				

Evaluations of Team Member Skill Level by Required Skill

	1	2	3	4	5	6	7	8	9	10	11	12	13	14	15	16	17	18	19	20
Team Members																				
Total of Above Ratings for Each																				
E																				
C																				
N																				

Rating system: E: expert; C: capable; and N: novice.

FIGURE 3.9 Team member skill levels

The histogram shown in Figure 3.10 is used to describe team member availability. If there's a conflict, more recruitment or training expenses may be discovered. At this point, the recruiting and training needs should be known and added to the budget. Training and recruitment also affect the cost of the team members. Highly skilled individuals earn more than their less-skilled colleagues. A resource histogram can help justify the need for a senior person. So can identifying the risk associated with hiring a less-skilled person.

	% Available	1. Conflict	2. Conflict	3. Conflict	4. Conflict
Team Members					

FIGURE 3.10 Resource availability.

Progressive organizations may maintain a cross-organization resource histogram that identifies and evaluates all worker skills. This is a fantastic tool. With it, I have discovered highly skilled, competent people in organizations that have let these workers flounder. The organizations assume that if a skill is not in someone's current job description, the worker cannot do it. Without a comprehensive approach to understanding your existing employees' skills, you'll lose those workers to other firms. You might also wrongly place confidence in inferior candidates who are effective self-promoters.

Each time a project is completed, team member competencies should be evaluated on the histograms. This lets managers fully understand the resources available to them. If you don't do this final step, you leave team members' strengths and weaknesses undocumented.

One organization I worked with had a software development manager who had weak technical skills. When conflict erupted on her team around the best way of approaching a software design, she was helpless. Lacking a better idea, she supported the team member she liked best. The consequences?

1. The team was not allowed to make its own decisions regarding the software approach, so only her favorite team member was happy. The manager could have used the insight that flows naturally when a team is allowed to work through its own issues, but she chose not to.

2. Two of her best developers quit. She laughingly told me she was happy they were gone, because she didn't want troublemakers on her team. This woman was the poster person for the Peter Principle. If the organization had previously incorporated team member evaluations or maintained a corporate skills matrix, she might have at least had a clue that her chosen one was merely a self-promoter with mediocre skills.

3. In her role as project manager, she should have been evaluating team members. By failing to do this, she picked poor designs and lost great people.

There will always be self-promoters, and project managers may need to change an "expert" designation to "capable" to improve future staffing decisions.

Teams may also have shrinking violets who consistently rate themselves at a lower level, so they don't appear arrogant. Project managers should bump up these workers' ratings.

A savvy project manager must prepare interview questions to evaluate the teams' expertise, as well as the skills of anyone being considered for employment.

As you conduct a project, you should be constantly evaluating the performance of each team member. When people do something well, let them know. If they do something not quite so well, you should let them know that too.

Incentives—Pure Brilliance

You cannot motivate team members to work harder, work faster, take fewer breaks, or cut down on the 70 percent nonproductive and nonworked time unless the members of the team decide it is in their best interest. The following is absolute brilliance in providing workable incentives.

The project involved building a major state bridge. Estimated daily toll receipts would total $84,000. The state budget needed the bridge to be completed on time, as the state was counting on this revenue stream to balance its budget. This was made very clear to the project manager. Every day the bridge construction was incomplete, the state would lose $84,000, plus the cost of having workers spend more time on the project.

The project manager got crafty. He offered the general contractor $50,000 for each day the project was finished ahead of schedule. The state would gain $34,000 for each day the project completed early, which was certainly better than the state's situation if the team missed its deadline.

The general contractor was wise enough to understand he couldn't just demand better performance, so he offered all team members and vendors a share of $35,000 for each day the project completed early. The general contractor would receive an additional $15,000 per day for early delivery.

The team members loved the opportunity to share $35,000 a day for early delivery. Morale soared. Members actively encouraged each other to keep working, stop talking, hurry up! The project was delivered 105 days early.

The project manager received no part of the bonus. This person understood the concept of capacity planning and, better yet, understood that incentives were the only way to get the project delivered on time, let alone early. The state benefited by $3.5 million, the general contractor received an additional $1.5 million, and the team members divided more than $3.6 million. Sadly, greatness is rarely recognized. The highway department leader was fired because the state had paid $5.1 million extra. The boss couldn't understand that the state had truly benefited by $3.5 million, over and above what had been paid out.

A subordinate project manager once asked me if she could use project money to buy pizza as a reward for her team performing well. My response was simply, "Based on what you know of me, what do you think my answer will be?"

The project manager responded, "You will say it's a fine thing to do as long as I included it in the budget as an incentive, right?" She understood me well. Even better, she had allocated money in the budget for exactly that purpose. That is an example of a mentor having a good day!

Summary

After you have incorporated all budget items into your estimate, your organization will benefit from greater confidence in how much the project will cost and how long it will take. In our strategic planning example, you will know the budget for implementing the CRM (customer relationship management system), conducting a global advertising campaign, and reorganizing your supply chain. However, since the budget methodology has now been modified, all formulas for evaluating performance based upon metrics have been thrown out the window. We must learn a new way of monitoring.

Monitoring Progress

Project managers often use red, yellow, and green to indicate project progress. This type of progress report is completely meaningless, yet present in more than 90 percent of all projects. Why? It's easy, subjective, and common. No one will call you out for using it.

To reach a more accurate understanding of exactly how each project and strategic objective is performing compared with its budget and schedule, a much more in-depth approach to metrics must be implemented. Figure 3.11 provides an example. The result is absolutely worth the effort.

Guidance	Budget	Estimate at Completion	% Complete	Variance
$200 Million	$50M	$49M	100%	+$1M
	$50M	$55M	35%	−$5M
	$100M	$90M	40%	+$10M
$300 Million	$100M	$99M	70%	+$1M
	$100M	$90M	22%	+$10M
	$100M	$105M	39%	−$5M
$500 Million	$200M	$180M	100%	+20M
	$200M	$210M	35%	−$10M
	$300M	$299M	40%	+$1M

FIGURE 3.11 System developed metrics.

Earned Value Concept

The traditional method bases monitoring on earned value. Simply put, as each project activity is completed, the estimated cost of that activity accumulates to what is called earned value. As the project progresses, this bucket grows, and a manager must continually compare it with the actual cost of performing those work activities. Directly comparing the accumulated estimates against the accumulated actual cost and noting any gap between the two provides accurate insight into the performance of budgets and schedules.

Example

The accumulated earned value (estimated cost of each completed activity) of a project is $26,000. The actual cost of the project thus far is $32,000. The project is currently $6,000 over budget. Traditionally, the project manager should project the cost performance index (CPI) over the life of the project to determine how the project will complete given its present course. In this example, $26,000 divided by $32,000 is 0.81, so that is the project CPI. If the budget for this project is $500,000, that number, divided by the CPI, determines what the project is currently expected to cost when finished. In this case, the estimate at completion (EAC) is $617,284. At the current pace, the project will finish $117,284 over budget, a number that's called the budget variance.

If the project manager tracking the costs has not added all the ETV of risk, changes to risk, meetings, or any of the other budget components that the traditional method doesn't consider, then the project's actual cost is likely closer to $50,000. This would make the CPI equal to 0.52. The estimate at completion is now $961,538, instead of the budget value of $500,000. The budget variance is now $461,538. Spread this out over the portfolio of projects for that strategic objective, and you can foresee the impending disaster.

The Traditional Method

The perfectly estimated and completed project would be one in which earned value equals the actual cost for work packages and activities only. Put another way, the traditional method would leave you with the results shown in Figure 3.12.

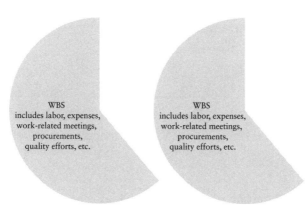

FIGURE 3.12 In a perfect budget, earned value will equal actual cost.

For this purpose, we must learn how to modify earned value techniques to include all the new budget components. The key to each is remembering that you earn what you estimated at the point that each activity is complete.

Status Meetings
Status meetings are estimated by the week—not by the meeting. To that purpose, earned value is gained every week, not every time a meeting is conducted. This means earned value occurs whether you held two meetings or none. If a meeting can be avoided, the project benefits, because you have earned value without any offsetting cost. Obviously, the efficiency of your meetings makes a significant difference.

As an example, say 30 team members earn $50 per hour and are scheduled for a two-hour weekly meeting. They will earn $3,000 whether the meeting takes two hours, lasts for four hours, or doesn't happen at all or if just three people show up. Again, the estimate is by the week, not by the hour or by how many attended.

Initiation and Planning

You should have completed initiation and planning costs before the budget is finalized. All costs of initiating and planning are earned with the beginning of project execution.

Project Manager

The project manager cost, as with the status meeting cost, is estimated by the week. This means the cost is earned even while the project manager is on vacation, sick, or otherwise unavailable.

Risk

Risk should be continually identified and proceed through qualitative and quantitative evaluation and risk response planning. The project will become more or less risky as the project proceeds. To depict this accurately, earned value from risk will increase or decrease over time. It is evaluated in comparison to the previous week's expected monetary value of risk.

We begin with the quantitative analysis form for a construction project (Figure 3.13). In this example, you can examine the qualitative analysis to see why the budget for risk was a little over $1.2 million.

Risk #	Risk Name	Impact	Likelihood	EMV	
1	Ground issues	$1,500,000	30%	500,000	
2	Steel supply	$800,000	42%	536,000	
3	Steel availabilty	$280,000	61%	170,800	
4					
5					
6					
				1,206,800	Total EMV– Budget Reserve

FIGURE 3.13 Qualitative analysis example.

Next we perform risk response planning. In the risk response planning document (Figure 3.14), it is easy to identify how earned value for risk is obtained. You can now see how this project's risk has been greatly reduced. Additionally, the budget included $1,206,800 for expected monetary value of risk. In this example, $160,000 was spent with an EMV reduction of $1,046,800, which now becomes earned value.

However, since risk is continually identified and efforts are taken to avoid, minimize, or transfer it, the best method to show earned value from risk is simply to subtract the EMV of this reporting period from the EMV of the last period. That value could be positive or negative. Through risk response planning, project managers may have their greatest impacts on projects.

In a traditionally managed project, the project manager does not have the authority to implement risk response planning unless each issue is taken through integrated change control. The reason for this is that doing this would allow work to be performed that is

Risk #	Risk Name	EMV	Risk Response	Mitigation Cost	EMV Reduction
1	Ground issues	500,000	Construct barrier	$80,000	$420,000
2	Steel supply	536,000	Secure secondary supplier	$35,000	$501,000
3	Steel availability	170,800	Buy now while supply lasts	$45,000	$125,800
4					
5					
6					
	Risk reserve	1,206,800		$160,000	$1,046,800

FIGURE 3.14 Risk response planning example.

not specifically approved. However, a clever project manager could create flexibility by specifically defining that flexibility into the project manager authority section of the project charter. If the expected reduction in risk through mitigation, for example, is greater than the cost of that mitigation, then approval should be a no-brainer. If the sponsor signs off on a project charter that includes those words, you do not have to worry about this limitation.

Meaningful Metrics

When your earned value and actual cost figures are realistic and based on the same definitions, the metrics suddenly gain usable meaning, and the defined metrics suddenly become valid. Some of these include:

- **Cost performance index.** Total earned value/total cost. This indicates estimate accuracy, where:
  - 1.0 indicates the project was estimated perfectly, which never happens.
  - >1.0 means the project is under budget.
  - <1.0 means the project is over budget.
- **Estimate at completion.** Budget/CPI. This indicates how much money the project should cost to complete, based on its current performance.
- **Estimate to complete.** EAC minus actual cost. This indicates how much money the project needs to finish, beginning now.
- **Budget variance.** EAC minus budget. This indicates the expected amount over or under budget.

You can see an example of a status report that contains many of these metrics in Figure 3.15.

CPI Cost Performance Index	SPI Schedule Performance Index	ETC Estimate to Complete	EAC Estimate at Completion	Budget	Variance
1.18	0.98	$55,000	$290,909	$320,000	$29,090
Project manager notes: A delivery delay caused a slight change to schedule. The project will finish roughly $29,000 under budget.					

FIGURE 3.15 Example of a meaningful status report.

Summary of Monitoring

Revamping your budget development method has a significant impact on your ability to monitor.

Think of project management that follows traditional methods letter for letter. When your budget contains only one bucket for doing the work of the project and one bucket for the EMV of risk, there's nowhere to put all the costs of a project manager, risk, initiating and planning, meeting times, and so on. Your actual cost will continue to hit the budget in the same way, but the method used to monitor that budget would produce terrible results, because you are not earning value on cost categories not included in the budget. Your actual costs will be much higher than estimated. Your estimate must include the earned value of these items to adequately reflect how your realistic project performance.

The ultimate in monitoring is now produced by UltiMentors' Ultimate PM software. Based upon the foundation described above, it will provide much better information than ever before available. Figure 3.16 provides an example of a strategic plan.

In this, we created the ultimate tool. We show all the critical metrics plus add some of our own. People should be able to compare the percentage of the budget spent with the percentage of the project completed. Also, we determine the internal rate of return (IRR) for projects as well as the strategic objective, are positive. An IRR greater than 1 means the project is still financially viable because the

Strategic Plan
Increase Sales Volume by 50%

Budget	Cost Performance Index	Estimate at Completion	Variance	Estimate to Complete	% Budget Spent	% Complete	Initial IRR	Current IRR
$24,721,794.00	0.81	$30,666,141.40	–$5,944,347.40	$22,643,878.81	26.16	22.70	1.24	1.16

Portfolio of Projects Delivering Strategic Plan
International Advertising Campaign

Budget	Cost Performance Index	Estimate at Completion	Variance	Estimate to Complete	% Budget Spent	% Complete	Initial IRR	Current IRR	Impact on Objective
$9,500,000.00	0.68	$13,970,588.24	–$4,470,588.24	$13,495,588.24	3.40	2.50	1.24	1.25	48%

Implement CRM

Budget	Cost Performance Index	Estimate at Completion	Variance	Estimate to Complete	% Budget Spent	% Complete	Initial IRR	Current IRR	Impact on Objective
$6,198,100.00	0.79	$7,860,842.81	–$1,662,742.81	$5,375,716.81	40.09	31.61	1.08	0.96	4%

Reorganize Supply Chain

Budget	Cost Performance Index	Estimate at Completion	Variance	Estimate to Complete	% Budget Spent	% Complete	Initial IRR	Current IRR	Impact on Objective
$9,023,694.00	0.95	$9,498,625.26	–$474,931.264	$6,269,092.67	35.00	34.00	1.28	1.28	48%

FIGURE 3.16 A strategic plan produced with UltiMentors' Ultimate PM software.

benefit is greater than the cost. A project can be performing badly by metrics, but still be worth finishing because it's still worth more to complete.

In Figure 3.16, the strategic plan shows a current IRR of 1.16, which means the project should continue because of the economic viability even though it's nearly $6 million over budget.

The software also can be used for decision making. If you look at the individual project of CRM, you will see that the project only has a 4 percent impact on the strategic plan and the IRR of that project is less than 1.0. Perhaps a decision to cut that project and relabel the strategic plan to "increase sales by 46 percent" would be called for.

Imagine those metrics belonging to General Motors and using this tool for strategic planning. All GM department budgets for projects could roll up from product lines such as Chevrolet, Buick, Cadillac, and so on. Then up to the corporation as a whole. This information could prove indispensable.

A bank could require customers to provide access to these metrics in return for a cut on interest rates, and it would give the bank great insight into how well its loans are being used. A state government could make this information available to taxpayers so they can see how well the projects were performing that they pay for with tax money.

All this is now available!

CHAPTER FOUR

How Long Will It Really Take?

A New Approach and More Accurate Results

Overview

At this point, you should understand how to:

- Dissect a strategic plan into strategic objectives, then into a portfolio of projects supporting each strategic objective.
- Break down all work necessary to accomplish each project, entering the information into a work breakdown structure (WBS).
- Estimate the effort and cost of each activity for each component of the WBS.
- Create an ironclad budget with all project costs included.
- Roll each of the costs in the ironclad budget back and upward into each strategic objective, then into the strategic plan itself.

- Monitor all budgets effectively with state-of-the art metrics.

Now it's time for the schedule.

What the Traditional Method Gets Right

Estimating time on the WBS is excellent. The way PMBOK describes making the network diagram is fantastic. Add the Gantt chart, and you can see a well-built schedule—in theory, perhaps. The reality is that the traditional method doesn't work the way it was designed for a couple of reasons.

How to Construct the Best Possible Schedule

Let's return to our deck replacement project (Figure 4.1). We began with the work breakdown structure, then estimated the time and cost of each activity, then rolled these costs up to each milestone and to the project as a whole.

We made a very large adjustment to bring reality into the equation based on capacity planning. Then we added the costs of meetings, initiating and planning, project management, the expected monetary value (EMV) of risk, and the expected time value (ETV) of risk. As opposed to the PMI budget of $19,325, we determined that the true cost of this project would be $79,920. The required hours for the schedule also ballooned from 317 to 1,057. The time spent managing, initiating, and planning the project has no effect on the schedule since we produced the schedule after planning was complete. We do need to adjust the time by the ETV of risk, which in this case adds an additional 5.3 days.

With that basic knowledge behind us, now it's time to learn to construct a realistic network diagram and show how that flows directly into creating an accurate Gantt chart.

We begin with taking the milestones and work packages from the WBS. In a small project, you can construct the network diagram

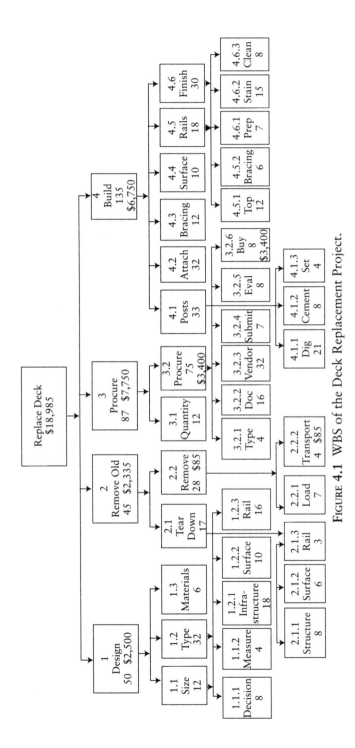

FIGURE 4.1 WBS of the Deck Replacement Project.

using only the work packages. For larger projects, you may show milestones only. The task is to use enough granularity to make it meaningful without rendering it unwieldy.

Before we begin to build the network diagram, it is essential to determine the most efficient method possible for the work to be completed. To do this, we must look at the nature of the work and understand the mandatory dependencies. For example, in our deck replacement project, we could not clear the debris away until after demolishing the existing deck. Simple logic can go a long way in organizing the work.

In our example—shown in Figure 4.2—A, B, C, and D may begin concurrently. Then:

- E follows D.
- F follows A, B, and C.
- G follows F.
- H and I can be performed simultaneously but must follow E and G.
- J follows H and I.
- K follows J.
- L follows K.
- Complete.

Remember, the critical path, which this shows to be 742.7 hours (93 days), also includes the ETV of risk. The traditional method does not recognize the time value of risk, but it is still quite important.

Building a Quality Schedule

At this point, our schedules are adjusted by capacity planning and with the ETV of risk.

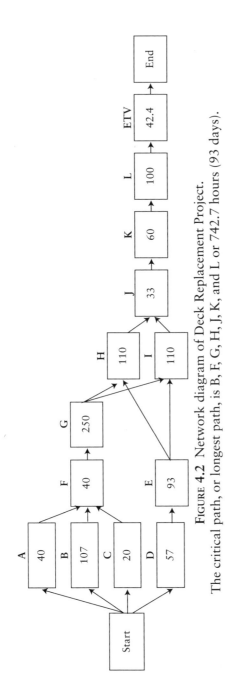

FIGURE **4.2** Network diagram of Deck Replacement Project.
The critical path, or longest path, is B, F, G, H, J, K, and L or 742.7 hours (93 days).

The critical path is crucial because it defines the length of the project. For this reason, the traditional method specifies that you should watch only the critical path, because any delay on the critical path will delay the project. That is true.

However, a system should monitor each path, at least in a tertiary way. A different path may be only a few days shorter. If a significant delay occurs on that other path, it might cause it to take longer than the critical path, thus creating a new critical path. Most project managers who use a network diagram (around 2 percent of total project managers) follow the initial critical path and never notice that a delay on a different path has changed the critical path.

Planned Value and the Scheduled Performance Index

Planned value is usually measured in dollars per week. It is computed by dividing the entire budget by the number of weeks in the critical path. This gives a weekly expected "burn rate."

For example, if the project budget is $2 million and the critical path is 20 weeks, the planned value is $100,000 per week. You expect to complete $100,000 in earned value each week. Therefore, the planned value for week 3 is $300,000. Comparing this number with an actual cost by week 3 of $320,000 (for instance) gives a scheduled performance index of 0.94. The traditional assumption is:

- A scheduled performance index (SPI) of 1.0 is right on time.
- An SPI of >1.0 means ahead of schedule.
- An SPI of <1.0 means behind schedule.

You'll need to know this to pass the PMP exam. Unfortunately, it doesn't work well in actual projects.

The reasons why SPI does not work include:

- It assumes there are no procurements. Let's use the same example as previously. In week 5, we bought a $1 million server farm. That purchase will skew the planned value for each week badly enough to make it meaningless. The best way to account for procurements is to find the specific week in the Gantt chart where the procurement will happen (week 5, in this case). Remove the $1 million cost from your calculations. Calculate that $1 million (half your $2 million project budget) divided by 20 weeks equals $50,000 per week. In week 5, when the procurement is expected, the planned value for that week will be $1,050,000. If the procurement is ahead of time or late, there may be a week or two of very strange numbers—but this is the only reasonable way to adjust for procurements.
- Other methodologies all maintain they cover every industry, yet assume there is an average workforce. Let's say this is a highway construction project. There will be huge fluctuations among team members in land moving, bridge building, concrete pouring, and asphalt laying and striping. How can a scheduled performance index be meaningful with a fluctuating team? I tried building a suitable mathematical model, but I finally decided that this was more complicated than it was worth.
- A project can have a scheduled performance index of perhaps 1.2 and be behind schedule. If the team spends more time working on activities not on the critical path than is prudent, the project may be late.
- Similarly, a project can have a scheduled performance index of 0.3 and be ahead of schedule. A procurement that isn't on the critical path may be delayed.

Scheduled performance index is a meaningful statistic if the project has no procurements, has a stable workforce throughout the project, and has a critical path that's so obvious, there is no chance that alternative paths will cause problems. Few projects fit this profile. Software development projects may occasionally hit the mark.

A much more accurate method for determining progress against the schedule is to monitor the schedule to actively manage the network diagram and Gantt chart. Mark times completed and monitor the critical path and other paths. With the Gantt chart, monitor whether work packages and activities are completed on time. This will give you a very good idea of how well the project is sticking to the schedule. The difficulty is that project managers, just like everyone else, want something simple to make their job a little easier. Simplicity sometimes creates its own problems, as in this situation.

Adjust the Network Diagram

Creating the best possible schedule involves modifying the network diagram. Begin by translating hours into days. We have already adjusted for capacity planning, so dividing by 8 for all hour requirements and then rounding up gives us the number of days required.

To determine that best possible schedule, follow these steps:

- Get ready to make that schedule. To do this, we need to figure out where we have flexibility (or slack) to delay something without delaying the project.
- The critical path tells us how long the project will take. Begin there to determine the earliest start date and finish date for each work package. Do this by adding corner information to our network diagram. As shown in Figure 4.3, each work package will be modified with ES (early start), LS (late start), EF (early finish), and LF (late finish).

- The reason you begin with the critical path is that it has no slack; a delay of anything on the critical path will delay the project. (Therefore, in every work package, the early start and late start of each are the same as the early finish and late finish in the case of each work package, as are the early finish and late finish.) You can see this on our modified deck project network diagram, shown in Figure 4.4.

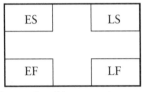

FIGURE **4.3** Example of how each network diagram should be altered to find slack.

Through forward and backward passes, we determine the earliest start date for each action and the earliest end date for the work packages on other paths. Forward passes work only on the top corners representing early starts and late starts. Backward passes work for the bottom corners showing early finishes and late finishes.

- Look at the forward pass for the path that begins with D and E. D can begin on day 1 at the earliest. If the work package takes 8 days to complete, then it makes sense that the early finish would be 9 (1 + 8). Work package E then could begin on day 9. If it takes 12 days, that work package would complete on day 21. Since H and I depend on both G and E, these work packages cannot start until the longest one finishes on day 33.
- Now examine the backward pass to determine finish dates. Because ETV ends on day 81 and takes 9 days, it stands to reason that the late start for it would be day 72, which means M can have a late finish of day 72, and so on. Work

118

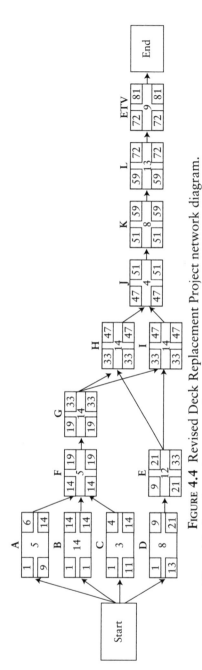

FIGURE 4.4 Revised Deck Replacement Project network diagram.
The critical path, or longest path, is B, F, G, H, J, K, and L or 742.7 hours (81 days).

package I has a late start of day 33, so E has a late finish date of 33. Now you can see some flexibility. E can finish anywhere from day 21 to day 33 and not delay the project. This could indicate where training, days off, and other rest periods can be scheduled.

When we spread out all these time periods on a Gantt chart with no dates, as we've done in Figure 4.5, we can get a fair understanding of our progress.

Meetings Impact on the Schedule

It's a simple job to schedule meetings on the Gantt chart. The easiest way may be to use the Gantt chart as input to mark weeks and change some durations as necessary.

For example, if the project is 30 weeks long and 2 hours are necessary each week for meetings, that adds 7.5 days to the schedule [(# of weeks times # of hours)/8, or $(30 \times 2)/8$].

In our deck replacement project, 4 people have a 30-minute meeting once per week, so we add one training day every 4 weeks. Multiply 4 workers by 30 minutes to get 2 hours per week. Multiply that by 4 weeks, and you have one extra 8-hour day per month in the Gantt chart. The project expanded by 4 days.

Therefore, the Gantt chart should be adjusted as it appears in Figure 4.6.

Our deck replacement project now has a schedule that includes meetings and has already taken the critical path into consideration, so no further changes are necessary on the network diagram. The project has expanded from 81 to 85 days. (The critical path is always in a different color, to distinguish it from the others and bring it to your attention.)

Although you can pay for a Gantt chart program, you don't need to. I did this with a simple spreadsheet, and it works well.

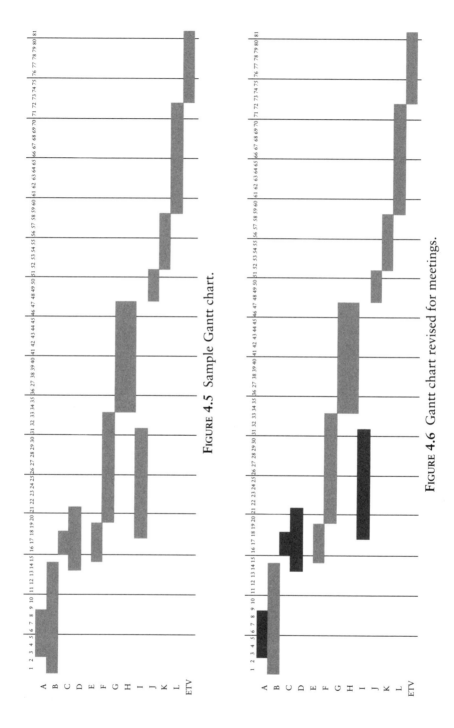

FIGURE 4.5 Sample Gantt chart.

FIGURE 4.6 Gantt chart revised for meetings.

Notice that, at this point, this schedule is different from all others because we've added the ETV of risk. It fundamentally changes the ball game by adding meeting time back into the schedule after the network diagram has been developed.

There is no reason to modify the network diagram to reflect meetings, because the network is built from a WBS that's been adjusted for meetings. I built this Gantt chart from the network diagram.

Also, when your project has a start date, days 1 through 85 on the Gantt chart are replaced by actual dates. That makes it easier to monitor.

The UltimatePM software, which my company created, automatically generates the network diagram, converts it into a Gantt chart, and modifies it with meetings. It generates everything and maintains it with real data. You can always see if you are on budget and on schedule, because the system does all the monitoring.

Fast Tracking Is More Than a Schedule Compression Tool

Fast tracking, generally considered a traditional project management tool used to catch up if the project is running late, involves finding as many tasks as possible to be performed simultaneously as opposed to sequentially. This can speed up the project and regain significant time.

However, fast tracking is more than a schedule compression tool, though that's how it's most often used. Its best use is in project planning. Here's why.

An exceptional project manager constantly examines the network diagram and questions whether dependencies between activities are mandatory or discretionary. She examines discretionary dependencies to determine whether fast tracking can help the project gain efficiencies, which can reduce cost and time.

For example, one former customer thought there were mandatory dependencies that forced the database to be completed first
(because middle-tier and front-end developers needed to know data
element names) and the middle tier second (because front-end developers needed to know data object names). Then the front end could
be developed. We changed that thinking by adding a design meeting.

Figure 4.7 shows the network diagram as originally designed by
the team. For a team of 12 developers, the project would have cost
$816,000.

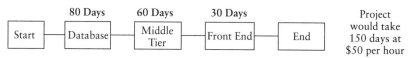

FIGURE 4.7 Former customer network diagram
for software development project.

As a senior-level project manager, I looked at the network diagram
with extreme skepticism. I mandated an all-team design meeting
where we described and named all the data elements we needed.
Then we defined and named all the necessary middle-tier objects.

In just two days, we eliminated the need for sequential development and moved completely to simultaneous development. You can
see the resulting change in the revised network diagram in Figure 4.8.
The cost of labor fell to $393,600—over half the previous amount,
while the duration dropped from 170 days to 82.

The two-day design meeting got everyone involved in naming
each data item and data object before any were developed. The middle tier knew the data element names and could program to call
them. The front-end developers knew the names of the data objects
prior to their development. When the people in the organization saw
the impact of my changes, they modified their software development
life cycle to fit the newly adapted process.

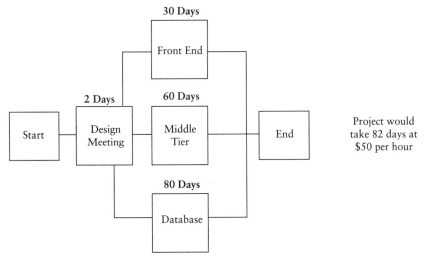

FIGURE 4.8 Revised customer network diagram for software development project based upon fast tracking.

You should constantly perform fast tracking, looking for ways to streamline the project. Don't wait until the project is in trouble and then look to fast tracking for a fix. It can be effectively used that way, but you miss so much by not planning from the beginning to use fast tracking for streamlining.

The project manager can provide the most value by streamlining the project wherever possible and (as we saw in Chapter 3) by performing risk response planning. (Much of the cost can be cut as a result of both streamlining and risk response planning.) In this way, superior project managers are worth every penny.

Summary

You have a budget and a schedule that are as accurate as possible. You understand how to monitor both effectively. You understand that project management can be significantly improved over the traditional method with budgets and schedules that reflect what is really needed.

CHAPTER FIVE

Procurements

Avoiding Contracting Disaster

The purpose of this chapter is not to provide an in-depth contract law course, but to examine specific issues that cause severe problems for projects and to provide unique and workable solutions for those issues. I've included enough information to protect against major issues relating to poorly conceived and executed contracts, as well as vendor relationship issues.

Laws Provide Protection
Against Selective Enforcement

Some years ago, I was forced to inform the director of a major state agency that his organization had no enforceable contracts.

The difficulty was created by a contract the agency chose not to enforce. The agency had a vendor that seriously underestimated a fixed-price contract. The agency decided to save the vendor's business from serious harm by paying that vendor more than the amount specified in the contract. There was no contract change order, nor was there a renegotiated contract. The agency just spent more money than specified in the contract.

This scenario should have ended with the contract canceled and the work rebid. This is to protect the organizations that bid the project correctly, but would be penalized if the poor bidder got the extra money and the good bidders lost out on fair competition.

When an organization fails to enforce a contract once, it invalidates all contracts. Other organizations could deliberately underbid a contract, then demand more money. If the organization refused, the vendor could sue, because it was not receiving equal treatment under the law. The vendor could simply subpoena contracts, and if it found a contract that hadn't been enforced to the letter, it could sue on those grounds.

The United States protects residents from selective enforcement. If 10 drivers are all speeding, an officer cannot just pick one car out of the line and give the driver a ticket. In court, the driver might ask, "Did it have to do with my race or my age?" These tickets are routinely thrown out.

Understand the implications of this part of the law. It can protect you.

Never Compromise Ethics for Any Reason

During my first major project, I led the selection of vendors for software, mainframes, cabling, and everything related to them. These were multimillion-dollar contracts.

One day the door to my office opened, and two of the most gorgeous women I had ever seen walked in, then locked the door. One of them pushed my chair back, straddled my lap facing me, and whispered seductively, "Duane, what will it take to get this business? We'll do *anything*!"

That's when my brain kicked in. I asked the woman if she wanted to know the secret of what it would take to get the contract. She said that was her purpose exactly.

I responded, "Then get off my lap, open the door, and give me the best price versus performance bid, and I will give you the contract."

Two and a half months later, I signed the contract for their bid. They competed the right way and won.

If I had taken them up on their illicit offer, I would have endangered my relationship with my family, given the bidder blackmail material, hurt my client, and probably lost my career.

Understanding Verbal Contracts

Many business executives and project managers understand that verbal contracts are binding. But they may not understand what the ramifications are or how to protect themselves.

It's common to have many discussions and even verbal agreements with a vendor before writing a contract. As a result, attorneys have helped executives understand that the written contract should state something along the order of "This contract supersedes all previous agreements."

The difficulty is that this wording does not apply to subsequent agreements: those that could be agreed to after the signing. Here is one actual scenario that shows the reason this is important.

An executive I know was sitting at his desk when he received a call from a vendor talking about what a wonderful day it was. The call went on for five or six minutes, and the executive thought nothing further about it until a few weeks later when he learned that the vendor had three employees listening in and all of them stated the executive and the vendor had agreed during the call to a 40 percent boost in contract dollars to account for the higher costs that the vendor was experiencing. Since this "agreement" was verbal and four vendor people "heard" him agree, the verbal contract was binding.

How does an organization protect itself from a fake agreement like this? Make a contract stipulation like this: "This contract can only be modified through a formal contract change order agreed upon, in writing, by both parties."

Privity

Privity is a frequently misunderstood term that can cause problems. It refers to contractual relationship partners. Here's why it's an important issue for you.

First, it's important to understand that, unless specified otherwise in the contract, contracts can be sold or given to another party.

Let's say Company A hires Vendor B to finish some work. Vendor B decides to sell the work to Vendor C to do the work (also called subcontracting). Company A has no control over Vendor C because those two organizations have no privity (contractual relationship). Only B can control C, assuming there's a contractual agreement between the two. Therefore, if Company A wants to always have contractual control, the contract must state that selling the contract is prohibited or specify that any subcontractor must agree to the stipulations of Company A. Even then, it's not an easy problem to avoid.

Breach

What constitutes breach should be specified in every contract. The remedy for breach must also be spelled out—otherwise, it's not enforceable. A good example of this occurred when I hired a company to do work for a customer of mine. I completely defined what constitutes breach in the contract.

The company I hired failed to perform adequately according to the contract, and I had to sue for nonperformance. The judge ruled in my favor and then said, "Because no remedy for breach is spelled out in the contract, I shall impose no remedy." Talk about a Pyrrhic victory! The company I hired was deemed to be in breach, and I received no compensation because I hadn't specified what the compensation should be. I never repeated that mistake.

When you discover a breach, immediately serve the breaching party with an official notice of breach. When the company in breach has been informed of the problem, courts will allow it a reasonable amount of time to fix the issue. Steps can be addressed based upon responses by both parties, but understand the intent of the notice of breach. In no way will courts allow one party to nitpick a tiny item and believe it cannot be required to pay. Courts routinely stop those "tricks" from being enforced.

One of my clients signed a contract with a vendor, and everything seemed fine until the end of the project when it was time to hand off the product the vendor was building for my client. Instead of handing off the product, the vendor gave us a notice of breach, saying that some *i* dotting and *t* crossing were missed by us and therefore we violated the contract and, even though we'd paid them, they didn't need to deliver anything. The court explained to the vendor that a notice of breach must be timely. We had to have the opportunity to correct the issue. This is a legal requirement. Since the notice of breach was obviously delayed so the vendor would be able to reap a greater profit, through getting regular payments but not actually completing the work, the court rejected the claims of breach and required the vendor to pay us damages for not completing the project as agreed. Courts look to what makes sense and to discern intentions. It was easy to see that the intention in this case was to take advantage of us.

Types of Contracts

Organizations and senior project managers must understand different contract types and how and when to use each one. I find that many deals use the wrong type of contract.

Overview

Overall, think about the incentives that each type of contract provides and decide how to protect the organization if those incentives could result in injury to the organization. Figure 5.1 provides some helpful pointers.

Cost-Plus-Fixed-Fee and Cost-Plus-Incentive-Fee Are by Far the Best in Most Situations

Cost-plus-fixed-fee and cost-plus-incentive-fee are the best contracts since there is no incentive to pad (assuming receipts are audited). These are the only types of contract that provide no incentive to cheat.

Cost-Plus-Fixed-Fee

In a cost-plus-fixed-fee contract, you and the vendor agree on the profit—the fixed-fee portion. You also reimburse the vendor, based on receipts, for project-related expenses.

A cost-plus-fixed-fee contract typically divides the fixed fee paid to the vendor by the number of periods expected in the project. If you are smart, you will only agree to pay up to 80 percent of that fee each period. You retain at least 20 percent to guarantee completion, specifying that funds retained will be paid when both parties sign off on project completion.

Issue	Fixed Price	T&M	Cost-Plus-Percentage-of-Cost	Cost-Plus-Incentive-Fee	Cost-Plus-Award-Fee
All scope defined	Good—but if you don't include everything such as meetings and status reports—you pay more because of change orders. Also, leads to overcharging as providers over-charge to compensate for risk associated with the fixed price.	Not good—cost unknown and typi-cally higher.	Unacceptable—vastly increased cost and risk.	Good because there is no incentive to overcharge, and there is reason to find ways to save money.	Good because there is no incentive to inflate costs.
Scope not completely defined	Not good—ham-mered with change requests.	Simple and easy—but necessary for much auditing since fraud is easy.	Unacceptable—vastly increased cost and risk.	Good because thee is no incentive to over-charge, and there is reason to find ways to save money.	Good because there is no incentive to inflate costs.

FIGURE 5.1 Contract pointers.

Maybe the project runs late, continuing 10 weeks longer than anticipated. If you've paid the vendor the entire flat fee, the vendor may decide that it isn't worth continuing the job.

For an example, imagine that your project is scheduled to last 50 weeks, and you are paying a vendor a flat fee of $250,000, to be paid in equal portions every 2 weeks. So you owe the vendor $10,000 every 2 weeks. At the end of 50 weeks, the vendor has the entire fee. You may still need to pay expenses, but the vendor might decide that it makes business sense to walk away from reimbursement.

But if you withhold 20 percent of each $10,000 payment, you'll still have $50,000 left to pay at the end of that 50-week schedule. That's a solid reason for the vendor to stay on the job until it is completed.

This type of contract works for both parties. The vendor knows exactly what its profit will be, the customer knows that the vendor has no incentive to pad receipts since the vendor was reimbursed only, and the vendor has an incentive to stay until project completion.

Cost-Plus-Incentive-Fee

This is just as good as the cost-plus-fixed-fee. It differs in that instead of paying only the agreed-upon fixed fee plus expenses, you agree to pay more when the vendor meets certain criteria.

Let's say you agreed to this type of contract, and it included a 5 percent incentive for every two weeks the project is completed early. There's a clear incentive for the vendor to work quickly and well.

Cost-Plus-Percentage-of-Cost

Some dreaded cost-plus-percentage-of-cost contracts are still kicking around. The US government was so ripped off by this type of contract that a law was passed to ensure the government could never again enter into this type of contract.

Yet states, local governments, and businesses continue to be assaulted by unscrupulous people with these horrendously nasty contract tricks. Make sure you're not their next victim.

Let's say the government uses a cost-plus-percentage-of-cost contract to build fighter planes. Since nobody knows what the costs will wind up being, the vendor tells the government, "How about you pay for our cost, plus 15 percent more for our profit margin?" This could sound great to the government. But then the vendor calls each of its suppliers and says, "Charge us four or five times as much as normal, and we will pay anything you want." This way the government's cost skyrockets in the same proportion as the vendor's profit. The incentive to inflate costs is huge.

Fixed-Price Contracts

This kind of contract is quite prevalent. The customer believes it reduces its risk of inflated cost and can get the best deal by forcing the vendor to live within a fixed amount. This leads to the following problems:

- Sellers, wishing to reduce their own risk, inflate the price. Therefore, the type of contract the customer thinks will save money generally costs more.
- Unless all work and all expectations can be clearly defined, there will be many change requests to add money for additional work.

Fixed-Price Contract Problem Example

When asked for a project status report, a vendor's project manager asked if status reports were specified in the contract. In this situation, they were not. The project manager then told the vendor, "If you wish to add status meetings to the contract, make a change request." He then tripled the hourly rate for these meetings.

When the buyer balked at this and reminded the seller the contract was based upon $50 per hour, the seller's response was, "Then find some other company that knows nothing about what is happening and pay it to run the meeting. The work is outside the contract."

Time and Materials

This is the most common professional services contract in use. It is great if you like paying people who fudge hours. While managing large projects for vendor organizations, I have been told to sign falsified time cards on three separate occasions by the companies I was working for. One of these resulted in criminal charges for one of the companies after I provided time cards and other proof of fraud to the government. I have never signed off on hours not worked. The difficulty is that padding hours is easy, efficient, and difficult to catch. In one government contract I worked on, fraud based on padding hours was significantly in excess of $1 million.

Summary

Project managers often choose the wrong contract type. Most organizations will opt for fixed price or time and materials, not understanding that there are serious, incentive-related problems with these choices. The best option is usually cost-plus-fixed-fee or cost-plus-incentive-fee. With either, there's no incentive to inflate. Understand privity and specify the ramifications of breach when writing contracts. Always stipulate that any contract change must result in a contract change order signed by both parties.

Last, remember to enforce all contracts to the letter, to avoid having all your contracts nullified due to selective enforcement.

CHAPTER SIX

Integrated Change Control

Integrated change control considers only the impact of changes to scope. The company described earlier, which used change requests to add budget to an undervalued project, was acting unethically. This chapter is about changes to scope that are entirely ethical. The issue is that sometimes either the project team, stakeholder, or sponsor may come up with an idea to improve the project that is greater than the scope of the project originally defined. Integrated change control is a method whereby the benefits and costs of making the change are addressed in a way that the organization can make a choice to accept or reject the change request.

In an agile environment, the organization never completely defines the project, so it will continue to change over time. As we discuss the process of unifying traditional and agile-type projects, the project must be completely defined—but can remain agile only with an active and simple integrated change control process.

Contrary to what I've seen in many organizations, the purpose of integrated change control is not to eliminate changes. The intention is to eliminate unnecessary changes.

The integrated change request process involves creating a change request. A project manager evaluates this request to determine the suggested change's effect on the budget, schedule, risk, quality, human resources, procurement, and capacity planning. Will the pros of accepting the requested change exceed the cost and any adverse changes to other elements? The organization uses integrated change control to decide for or against authorizing the work.

The best way to determine the effect of a change request is to go back to the WBS (work breakdown structure) and break down the work that needs modification—what steps will it involve? Next, reestimate revised work packages, activities, and potential milestones, using the entire budget and schedule process to understand the effect. Then evaluate whether your people have the bandwidth and skill sets to accomplish the work. If not, add to the human resources whatever is necessary to either build or buy (training your staff or bringing someone else in). Add those costs to the budget. Say yes only if the impact of the change is less than the benefit of making the change.

There have been many times over the years that I've had team members make decisions to add functionality without going through integrated change control. I warn them from project onset that this action will result in their termination if it is discovered. Here's why.

First, understand that the scope of the project has been signed off by the buyer. Even though the team member may attempt to justify the addition of functionality by saying, "The change took no time and cost no money," that's impossible. There is nothing we will ever do in this life that will cost no time or money. If the team member could complete the project on time and on budget and include the change, he still shouldn't. One reason is that the customer never agreed to the change and may not want it. Another is that the team member may have been able to deliver the project a little earlier, or the project might have cost a little less. All team members should understand this concept and only do what was approved or author a change request of their own to get the work approved.

A modification may be overvalued, depending on who is doing the evaluation. We saw that earlier when we talked about project justification. Do your best to ensure the number used has been adequately challenged.

Of course, there's more to integrated change control than just making the decision. It involves tracking the change requests; having a process for evaluating the impact of the change against the budget, schedule, and risk; and reporting the difference in a way that can lead to a decision.

This rigorous approach contrasts with the integrated change control I've most often seen in practice. In my experience, even in extremely large organizations with mature processes, integrated change control is usually a process where some leader compares an offhand estimate of the additional work against an equally offhand estimate of the advantage of doing this work and then putting the decision in the hands of a change board.

Ultimate PM, the proprietary software developed by my company, UltiMentors, lets the user input a change request. The system generates a number and then creates a new generation of the project. If Project.1 was the first iteration of the management plan, Project.2 is the new version, this one incorporating the change request. The software modifies the WBS and all the gyrations involved in every downstream adjustment this change would create. The proposed plan is presented to management. If the answer is yes, the system stores the most recent generation as the working plan and archives the original. If the answer is no, the system continues the original as the active plan and archives the failed change request information.

The New Paradigm for
Integrated Change Control

UltiMentors, my company, has introduced a new methodology that completely changes the process through a combination of industrial engineering and BPR (business process reengineering).

Let's use the example from Chapter 4, where we changed the software development life cycle to include design meetings in which all team members agree on the names of database elements and middle-tier objects prior to any work beginning. This change needs to be documented completely through BPR in the form of an As Is process flow document such as the one shown in Figure 6.1. At this point, the To Be workflow document, shown in Figure 6.2, also needs to be created.

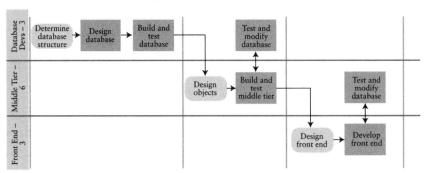

FIGURE 6.1 As Is software development life cycle.

Now that the processes are determined, there are two ways to determine the As Is and To Be time frames.

- One utilizes a WBS approach with the team members estimating the time and cost each step will cost. Since estimating is simple in this particular case, this approach should be used. It also should be used because of the low

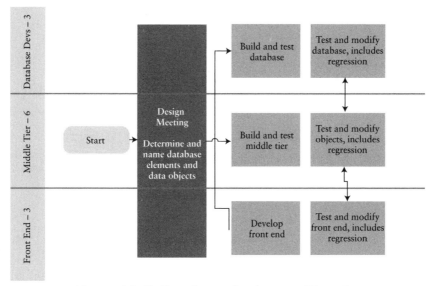

FIGURE **6.2** To Be software development life cycle.

frequency of doing projects—and accuracy in terms of days is fine. Should the frequency be high, an industrial engineering approach needs to be taken.

• In a more complex situation or one of high repetitions, with numerous process changes, work measurement as part of industrial engineering should be utilized where one can see precisely how long the time difference will be.

Now the As Is and To Be documents are modified to reflect the time requirements, shown in Figures 6.3 and 6.4.

Now the change can be computed in cost:

$$\text{As Is} = 150 \text{ days} \quad \text{and} \quad \text{To Be} = 82 \text{ days}$$
$$150 \text{ days} \times 8 \times 12 \text{ developers} \times \$50/\text{hr} = \$720,000$$
$$82 \text{ days} \times 8 \times 12 \text{ developers} \times \$50/\text{hr} = \$393,600$$
$$\text{Savings} = \$720,000 - \$393,600 = \$326,400, \text{ or } 57.4\%$$

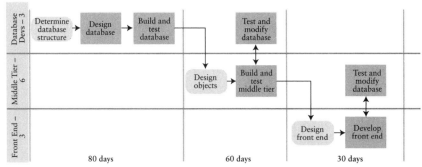

FIGURE 6.3 As Is software development life cycle
with time requirements added.

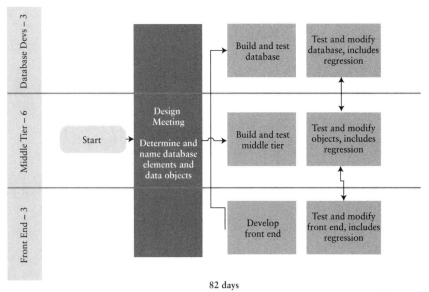

FIGURE 6.4 To Be software development life cycle
with time requirements added.

With this approach, now a change request can have the bottom-line savings quantified, so the decision to accept the change request should be simple.

In more complex examples, one may choose to incorporate the internal rate of return computations or net present value after projecting costs and savings over a four- or five-year period.

Other Use for Industrial Engineering

In Chapter 3 on budgets, we discussed capacity planning where, across industries, the average nonproductive time and nonworked time add to a total of 70 percent of all work time we pay for. This caused us to adjust all available work hours by 0.3. However, different organizations and different cultures may have significant variances from this figure.

Rather than just accept that 0.3 selection, you may choose to actually study the work in an organization and use the figures from that organization. For this particular type of study, there are two concepts to worry about:

- **Randomness.** Should you choose to take observations every five minutes, those being studied will plan for when they will look busy. This will totally skew the results. Therefore, never use a set interval between observations.
- **Randomness, part 2.** Never allow people to know who is being measured at any time. This is why I will go to the first desk but check and measure the person sitting to the left or right instead. To ensure randomness, perhaps rotating from observing the one to the left of the person or right is a good idea. In any event, the people being studied should not know they are the ones being studied.

Narrow your study to 10 percent of all work groups, with 10 percent of each group member studied and no fewer than 200 observations each. Use a tablet for your observations, and mark each observation with a W (= worked), NW (= nonworked), or NT (= not there). If the person you are observing is in conversation or on a device, spend the time necessary to determine if it's part of work. For example, if the person is talking about a football game even during a business meeting, the observation would be NW.

After the study, divide the total number of observations by the number of W observations to determine the percentage of time worked. For example, if 100,000 observations were taken and 40,000 W recordings occurred, that would be 40 percent.

The next meeting should be at the personnel office where the HR department should be asked about vacations, sick days, holidays, and mandatory training days.

Should all those numbers be entered into Ultimate PM, the correct percentages will be calculated automatically to be used in capacity planning.

CHAPTER SEVEN

Agile

Awesome? Or an Excuse to Keep People Employed?

The traditional project management methodology has morphed many times over the years with the present method referred to as PMBOK (Product Management Body of Knowledge). This methodology begins with initiating where the project manager is selected and the project is authorized by the organization. The initiation stage is completed after the project manager meets with the sponsor to generate basic information about the project in a project charter form.

When the project charter is formally approved, the planning stage begins. In this stage, the work is broken down into the WBS (work breakdown structure), times and costs are estimated, risk is examined, and all tasks necessary to prepare a budget and schedule are determined. At this point, the organization usually holds a kick-off meeting.

The team performs the work in the executing stage. The monitoring and controlling stages are performed simultaneously where the work is being done, and testing is performed until all work is completed, which begins the closing stage.

When the result of the execution is completed, the product of the project should be formally accepted. Until that product is accepted, the project remains in execution status. There is no completed work available until all of the product is completed.

The benefit of a well-planned and well-executed project should be its completeness and the way the product conforms to the needs of the organization. However, all that planning costs much time. Born out of the software industry, competing agile methodology arose and died. The current version of agile is generally referred to as scrum.

Agile development begins with almost no documentation whatsoever. The objective is speed. The team breaks down work into deliverable cycles generally of two to eight weeks. At the end of each cycle, code is pushed into production, and that piece of developed product is now available for use. This means an organization can generate much faster results. At the end of each cycle (sprint), a short meeting is held to choose what functionality will be created in the new sprint.

The obvious advantage of an agile methodology is that beneficial changes are recognized fast.

The best way to introduce agile—or scrum—is to use a valuable example I was lucky enough to witness (Figure 7.1).

While standing on the deck of a cabin on Hood Canal close to Hoodsport, Washington, I saw an occupied hummingbird nest in a limb just off the deck. Amazed as I was seeing such a sight for the first time, my lesson had just begun. A bald eagle landed in the tree just to the left of the tree with the hummingbird. I was in awe and stood as silently as I could because both were less than 20 feet from me. I just wanted to stand still, enjoy the moment and not cause either to want to leave.

FIGURE 7.1 An example of agile.

When the eagle took off, it began a large swoop in the direction of the hummingbird's tree, which caused the mother hummingbird to attack, perhaps out of fear for her family!

Yes, the world's smallest bird attacked America's symbol of power!

The tiny bird showed incredible agility as it continued to drive its sharp little beak into the eagle, pull out then stab it in again. The eagle could respond only in powerful and slow motions as the hummingbird continued its lightning fast attack. In and out, in and out with an eagle obviously not liking this situation at all. USA's national symbol of power was totally defeated and began to flee with the hummingbird fast on its trail, continuing the onslaught!

This experience can be interpreted as the perfect analogy for the importance of agile. Consider PMBOK as the eagle.

Agile for Project Management

Make no mistake, agile is the new buzzword. Many organizations have little idea what it is, but they are told that they need it and must become . . . agile. There seems to be a religious war in the project management world, with disciples of both agile and PMBOK openly disrespecting each other, leaving organizations totally confused about which direction to go.

As of 2018, of all the companies developing software, 97 percent employed agile in one form or another. Though there are several agile methods, scrum is by far the most popular, so I will give descriptions based on scrum.

Agile simply refers to agility. Agility refers to the ability to continually refocus direction and change as the situation requires.

As a cell phone manufacturer prepares for a future release functionality, the world seems to know about it in advance from leaks that somehow always happen about cell phone functionality prior to its release. In any event, the industry is so agile as a whole that a leak can enable a competitor to develop and release that same functionality, often before the original company. Now that is agility at its best!

What company would not like the agility to perfect that kind of competitive move? Scrum gives the ability to bob and weave in the competitive fights with unexpected counterpunches. Scrum provides that quickness and responsiveness.

The cell phone manufacturing industry is extremely agile, as people constantly upgrade their phones, wanting to have the latest and greatest in their hands and, sometimes, no matter the cost. Now consider the automobile manufacturing industry. Years ago, the public anxiously awaited new car releases because each year automobile manufacturers created unique designs and features that excited buyers. Today, because manufacturing costs have risen so much, most cars look very similar to all other cars on the market, and new designs appear but once or twice a decade.

Currently, electric car manufacturers have adopted agile, but the other carmakers have not. I bought a 2014 Mazda 6, which was a beautiful, wonderful car in my opinion. In 2020 that Mazda 6 is nearly an exact duplicate of the 2014 model. That's because the car is selling, and the cost of designing and releasing something new is too high to justify making changes. Other than a tiny appearance change, the only other modification has been to the software that updates it. Yet updates to software is backward compatible, and my 2014 has the latest updates.

The automobile industry is the antithesis of agility, except now in the electric car and alternative fuel parts markets, where they battle with agility for the crème de la crème of the market. These are generally expensive, high-end cars.

In agile, useful benefits are routinely developed. Since work is prioritized constantly based upon return on investment (ROI), organizations utilizing agile receive significant benefits regularly, with the most valuable constantly done first. This is as opposed to PMBOK projects, where benefits are received only at the end of the project—sometimes after the business need for the project has long since passed. Think of it this way: if a traditional project lasts two years and during that time a competitor has beat you to the market, that's a huge risk. There are times when changes in technology, such as a change of the Java JDK (development environment), have eliminated the need for you to build a software tool to accomplish the same.

There's almost no planning in agile, since the agility is so important. At the beginning of the project, the development team puts together a "backlog" list of all the functionalities that the organization's product owner provides. In scrum, the role of this product owner is to represent all the stakeholders of the organization. These ideas are generally not fleshed out. It's that person's responsibility to ferret out all requirements as the project is in process. Every two to eight weeks more backlog items are selected by the team—the hope is, with the support of the product owner—and developed.

Should business changes such as a competitive opportunity occur, the product owner generally notifies the team that creates backlog changes, and the priority of which functionality to add next is modified. This demonstrates agility.

As you can see, there's no way to easily develop a budget or schedule, because the work to be completed is a constantly moving target. This is both the value and the price of agility. There is virtually no project documentation, only historical records showing the velocity (the agile term for speed of progress), sprint burndown documents (the agile term for completion of the long list of functionalities) displaying the progress on each task as it gets completed, and the prioritized backlog describing desirable future functionalities.

The entire metrics section of SBOK (Scrum Body of Knowledge) is laughable. SBOK seems to come out of nowhere, seems to be copied completely from PMBOK, and has absolutely no description of methods to make it happen. The reason? It cannot realistically happen! How can you have metrics to show how the project is performing against the plan—when there is no plan! Ludicrous! If you do not have a complete understanding of scope, and do not build an effective budget and schedule to accomplish the entire project, then how on earth can you utilize metrics to determine where you are according to that fictional plan? Having that entire section in SBOK seems like a somehow pathetic attempt at validity.

There must be real planning for this to occur. You need to have requirements, build scope, and determine costs to build a budget and a schedule—and you need a method to make a valid comparison between the budget and actuals. To develop an ironclad budget, you must give up some flexibility, as described later. What good are metrics if you don't have a base to build from? They're meaningless!

As I discussed in Chapter 2, the definition of a project is a temporary endeavor undertaken to create a unique product or service. Projects are different from regular work in an organization, because unlike regular work, projects have a defined beginning and end— they have a limited duration.

In agile, projects aren't really projects. For an agile team developing a corporate website, that work may go on forever. There's always some useful functionality that can be added. If this is the case, the project is really regular work just managed as though it were a project.

It's okay to manage regular work like an agile project. Many manufacturers, such as Boeing, treat an order like a project and manage it that way. Yet what Boeing does is assemble aircraft, and so managing an order through PMBOK methodologies is fine. We just cannot refer to this as project management.

Agile Advantage

With agile, companies recognize continuous benefits. In PMBOK projects, the entire project is completed before the company realizes any of the benefits of conducting the project. If the project lasts longer than a year, sometimes the business reasons for completing the project become obsolete.

Modifying a PMBOK project involves formal change control. Though it's intended to protect the project from unnecessary changes, this adds times and money.

Agile Disadvantages

Agile has multiple disadvantages:

- Agile does not support strategic planning as easily as PMBOK because there is never a budget or a scope—and that's because there is no planning. The team selects different work for completion every two to eight weeks. How does one assign a cost or schedule to this? How do you determine ROI when you have no idea what work will be completed every two to eight weeks? Further, if there is no defined functionality of the end product, an agile project has no end.

- As a vice president of one of the world's largest online retailers once told me, "Agile is a scam to keep software developers employed. Agile projects never die. Once a team is in place, they always do something useful, but when we hire a team, we find they will be employed forever." Again, do you develop capital budgets for scrum teams or include the work in operational budgets, recognizing that the work is regular work? While I believe there is an important aspect to managing regular work as if it were a project, agile is necessary to help an organization keep certain products at a competitive advantage. This is because of the agility to modify the product quickly since it was never fully defined.

- How can you give a status report regarding how the project is doing against the budget or schedule when there is no budget or schedule, and you have no intention of ever reaching an end?

Certain types of projects fit one methodology more than the other.

The SBOK Guide describes how teams can use agile in any industry or project of any kind, because projects can just scale larger and larger. Many scrum teams can work on a single product.

The issue is total impracticality.

Let's say your organization is a highway development construction company. You cannot just base your project bid on continuous development and say, "Trust us, we'll figure out what we are going to do, how we will do it, and how much it will cost later." You must have a budget number to know how to bid. This requires planning, and the client usually agrees to those plans, instead of a scrum team deciding for itself how it will accomplish something. For this reason, traditional project management is the only way to manage these types of projects.

Also, scrum projects need steady team members who learn how to work together. Think about that highway construction project. The first team deployed is made up of the people with heavy earth movers and the truck drivers who carry away debris. The next team will work on bridges and the like. People with completely different skill sets perform each type of work. Scrum would not be effective, because you could not take advantage of any of its strengths. Also, we can't determine ROI on one part alone, because we must accomplish everything, or it is worth nothing.

Now turn to the business of software development. The team remains the same, and deliverables can be easily prioritized. This is the perfect situation for agile.

If you are building a new civilian airplane model, the software teams can be doing their work at the same time the wing makers are doing theirs. Even though their skill sets are different, they can at least be grouped. A new military airplane wouldn't be as natural a fit for agile. How do you develop an agile approach with government regulation specifying that you accomplish certain work in one way only? Strict government controls would cause significant problems for agile teams.

In airplane manufacturing, scrum teams end when their specific role is completed. For this reason, airline and other major manufacturers generally pair more favorably with PMBOK. However, airline and other manufacturing truly include very few projects. Where is the unique result? They can manage regular work through a PMBOK-like approach, and that's fine. Just never assume that fulfilling an order for airplane manufacturing can be a project, because it's regular work. It's what the organization does that matters. Perhaps when the airplane manufacturer builds a new model, the design, testing, and so on, of the first plane is a project, but I would even say that doesn't work, because designing and creating new models are also regular work for the company. It's what it does.

For a cell phone manufacturer, nothing about new releases is a project. It's all regular work that seems wholly compatible with agile. Most functionality involves software, but people working on cameras, security, and so on, will be the same teams working continuously to generate fixes, upgrades, and new product releases. Using PMBOK would greatly increase the time to market, because of all the planning necessary. Worst of all, you'd have to wait until all the work was completed before realizing any benefits. This is a perfect work environment for agile—and not projects.

Can PMBOK Projects Be Modified to Become More Agile?

Organizations should not have to be labeled as following either agile or PMBOK. As we've seen, agile should be used for regular, ongoing, technical work. PMBOK helps accomplish strategic planning that involves budgets and schedules, generally for nontechnical work. Why does it need to be one way or the other? There is an alternative: a method where PMBOK projects can be managed with agility and deliver regular improvements, and where agile can work quite well for projects and fulfill strategic planning by having budgets, schedules, and a fixed scope.

Managers should determine and analyze all necessary work through PMBOK by using the WBS. Develop estimates and budgets in the same way I've defined in Chapters 3 and 4. Rather than breaking the work down into work deliverables and using these as your milestones in the common PMBOK method, break the work down into two- to eight-week sprints, with the deliverable at the end of both the sprints and the overall project realized.

Now you have a fully planned project capable of fulfilling strategic planning objectives while delivering constant benefits. In addition, since each milestone has the same duration, one can modify the order of the milestones without impacting the budget or schedule. This would mean the backlog could be prioritized based upon return on investment (see Figure 7.2).

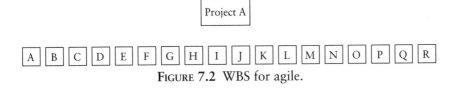

FIGURE 7.2 WBS for agile.

In this example, this small project has all the backlog agreed to ahead of time, with a budget and a schedule. If these milestones are 6 weeks long and there are 10 people on the team all making $50 per hour, that means $120,000 for each milestone. With 18 sprints, the budget is $1,920,000. We can modify the schedule simply by changing the order of the milestones. As we complete each milestone, we receive earned value of $120,000. If we finish only part of a sprint, we calculate what portion is incomplete and then subtract the value of that work from $120,000 total value. Let's say the team assessed completion at 90 percent during its sprint review meeting. Therefore, $108,000 was earned value, and the $120,000 was actual cost. This is the easiest, most efficient way to make agile work with strategic planning. The method can also merge with PMBOK. This is so much more complete than SBOK, which just provides monitoring formulas with no method to achieve any of it.

Also, there is a definite beginning and a definite end. We can make and meet budgets and schedules, use metrics, and monitor dashboards with this method.

Not thinking of PMBOK and agile as mutually exclusive is the key. Your organization can and should use both.

As I discussed earlier, any attempt to merge the two methods will require a robust integrated change control method. This allows constant modification, which enables agility but also pushes the organization to determine if changes to functionality modifications are worth making changes to budget and schedule.

Perhaps a revised change management system could automatically approve change requests where the return on investment is positive. This would require near total empowerment of the scrum product owner. We've already explored the notion that benefits, in any cost-benefit evaluation, can be overstated and in fact are overstated regularly, depending on the whim of the project sponsor. In this case, a scrum product owner could be held accountable.

CHAPTER EIGHT

Project Resources

The Science Behind Herding Cats

Hiring the Wrong Project Managers

I'm rarely more shocked than when I see who gets hired as project managers. The following steps outline a typical scenario for selection of a project manager for a large, mission-critical software application.

- After much thought, a job announcement is created. The company decides to look for someone who has managed large software development projects in the past.
- The announcement is submitted to recruitment organizations, which review applications and narrow down the choices to several applications from software development managers or lead developers who, in their opinion, managed development projects in the past. These applications are sent on to the business executives of the company looking for the project manager.

- The business executives are convinced that a particular applicant has great experience and knows a lot about developing large software projects, so the person is hired.

What's wrong with that scenario? Does it sound like this person is qualified to do the job? If so, you will repeat the same mistake these people made.

First, the person taken may have been a subject-matter expert (SME) regarding building software applications. That's great! However, the project will fail because the SME the company needed was a project manager SME.

An expert project manager would have been able to organize, plan, and lead a team to establish a budget, schedule, and everything else described to this point in the book. Yes, if the project is software development, the project manager subject-matter expert should also understand and use agile methodology, because the organization will need those continuous enhancements. However, this person never needed to be an expert on software development or website development projects. Instead, she knows how to use team members and software development SMEs to help plan and execute the project.

By hiring a software developer SME, you successfully repeated the Peter Principle. You have a highly skilled developer managing a project. Let's examine the skill sets.

- People skills are necessary for leading a team. Most developers became developers because they enjoy spending time and effort with a computer—usually, in my experience, more than they enjoy being with people. This is not a career populated with a high percentage of people-oriented professionals. Managing a team requires interpersonal and leadership skills not generally associated with software development.

- Only a highly trained project manager can accomplish the methods set out in this book. Do you want an ironclad budget and schedule? Do you want to know precisely how much your project will cost and when it will be completed? If not, hire your developer.
- Do you want to have meaningful status reports complete with the metrics specified in this book? I believe the answer to those questions is yes, so don't hire the developer.

Sadly, I see a high percentage of project managers who have no clue how to accomplish projects because they were the result of the Peter Principle. That's not to say that some of them cannot make the transition, but they cannot make that transition if they have the wrong personality type for the job, if they'd truly rather be developing software, or if they do not receive proper training.

Once I was interviewed for a job by an organization that wanted its project managers to also be coders: part-time developers and part-time project managers. This is a disaster waiting to happen. When the project gets to crunch time, when the most development is needed, it's also the time when the project management needs are at their greatest. Now you have a person with one foot in each world who will be unable to adequately perform in either. Also, think of the differences in personality types. One is a people person, while the other is typically the opposite.

Most organizations have limited resources and a fiduciary responsibility to protect their assets as much as possible.

Unfortunately, their mission-critical projects are being managed by people with little ability to accomplish that mission. Sometimes that results in a slow, agonizing slide into the abyss.

How Do You Find an Expert Project Manager?

How do you locate expert project managers, people capable of molding a group into a team and providing the expertise described so far?

I begin with the PMP certification. The PMP certification is not bad. It just isn't enough.

If this person will be managing a technology project, such as software development, then an SBOK certification, such as SMC (Scrum Master Certified), will at least be a base.

I ask a lot of questions:

- Tell me about a failed project you managed and what you learned from it? To this day, when I ask people this question, about 80 percent of respondents say they've never managed a failed project. This response indicates they have never really managed a project, are dishonest, or have no clue what success looks like. Which of those alternatives scares you the most? An honest appraisal of what a person did wrong goes a long way toward determining if this is the right person. I became an expert project manager because I learn from mistakes. Projects fail if they are completed over cost or over schedule. As you've seen, it's virtually impossible to determine how much time or money a major effort will take by following PMI guidance (or really anything else). Managers who say they've never managed a failed project just tell me they will fail if I hire them.
- How do you plan a project? If people do not include a WBS and a network diagram, the project will be managed haphazardly at best, as they have no clue regarding the fundamental base of knowledge necessary.
- How do you determine the budget? I presented a full description of how to do this. The candidate should hit at least some of the points.

Also, beware of hiring a candidate who is an expert in agile methodology. This person is an expert in developing software via an agile approach, such as scrum. PMBOK has given in to the demands of its people who were losing jobs to agile development gurus when it was not necessarily a great fit all the time. So PMI now offers an agile methodology. On one hand PMI describes what a project is, and agile doesn't fit that definition at all—the end result must be unique, and the work has a definite beginning and an end. Yet again, agile projects begin and rarely end, resulting in a much greater cost than anticipated when the project began.

How does this compare with the software expert managing a project? Does that person understand how to get requirements or how to construct a WBS, budget, or schedule? Generally, a software SME pretender will give you an offhand estimate of budget and schedule, using nothing more than guesswork. If this is the level of professionalism you're looking for, then you're the reason the project fails.

Leadership

According to a 2014 Gallup poll of executive board members, executives hire the wrong person 82 percent of the time. Perhaps the biggest impact of these poor hiring decisions is that fewer than 30 percent of American employees feel they work to their potential. This number is even worse globally, where that number is 13 percent. The biggest reason for this, employees say, is uncertainty regarding leadership expectations.

Just 18 percent of executive leaders are defined as "engaging" leaders. Engaging leaders inspire teams to work to their capabilities. Employees feel empowered and motivated. They are much more productive than average, with fewer defects, higher customer satisfaction, lower turnover, less absenteeism, higher profitability, and fewer safety incidents.

If 82 percent of executive hires are the wrong hire, the flip side is that 18 percent are engaging leaders who motivate and inspire employees to work to their capabilities. Of the 82 percent who are not engaging, only 20 percent are capable of changing. The others have the wrong types of personality.

Engaging leaders are critical to organizations—those 18 percent are responsible for 48 percent of organization profit. Imagine the impact if all executive hires were engaging leaders!

Why were the wrong executives hired?

- They were promoted out of positions at which they excelled (a familiar topic with project managers).
- They held a similar role at another company.
- They made a powerful impression on those doing the hiring, who wanted a decisive leader.

In regard to this last point, the question is, if the people doing the hiring value decisiveness over empowerment, does that mean they are looking to hire a clone of themselves? The reason I ask this is because choosing someone decisive is decisive. Unfortunately, a decisive leader generally is also a divisive leader, not a listener. What this essentially means is that these executives ascribe to McGregor's Theory X.

Douglas McGregor was a social psychologist who defined management personality types of Theory X and Theory Y. Theory Y executives believe workers are generally people who want to do good work and excel on the job. Theory X managers essentially believe people are slackards.

Theory X managers generally believe that:

- Workers will always try to do as little as possible.
- Employees must be treated harshly to be attentive to their duties.

- Employees cannot be trusted, especially when working on their own.

Curiously, those managers are always proved correct, because employees live up or down to their managers' expectations.

McGregor's Theory Y managers believe:

- Under the right conditions, most employees perform well.
- People are an organization's most important asset.
- Workers who derive satisfaction from their work will strive to do their best.
- People can take responsibility and, if allowed, will creatively solve problems. They don't need to be shadowed constantly.

Theory Y managers treat people with respect and develop a participatory, democratic leadership based on self-direction, self-control, and little external control. Theory Y managers are much more successful.

Having worked with many leaders, boards of directors members, CEO types, and so on, I would say decisive is the characteristic that defines nearly all of them.

Faruk Sahin's LMX Theory Managers Are the Best

LMX theory describes how leaders develop unique relationships with each employee. The quality of that relationship determines the effectiveness of both the leader and the employee.

Subordinates develop feelings of effective commitment when they feel managers treat them as important to the organization. Management style varies based on the relationship between supervisor and employee.

In adopting LMX theory, an organization attempts to create a symbiotic relationship between manager and employee, wherein the employee can attain Maslow's needs for self-actualization and esteem. When this happens, employees feel they are an important part of the solution and feel empowered to work for the betterment of the organization.

Engaging leaders have similar characteristics. They:

- Motivate employees to take actions and engage in compelling organizational missions
- Exercise assertiveness to drive outcomes and overcome adversity
- Create a culture of accountability
- Build relationships that create trust, dialogue, and transparency
- Make decisions based on productivity, not politics

In essence, they inspire, respect, reward, thank, and treat employees as valuable assets, and the result is highly motivated people.

What are the highest motivating actions you can take as a manager?

- Demonstrate to people that the organization and you, their manager, care about them professionally. This is especially true if you help them set long-term goals for professional growth and work to help them achieve those goals.
- Demonstrate to people that the organization and you care about them personally. Sometimes this is accomplished just by asking people how they are doing and listening to their responses. Show interest in them, their families, and so on.
- Be actively involved with the team and help the team members work together to achieve a goal for the organization. Encourage the team members to work together to resolve issues and become more productive.

- Empower employees by giving them the authority to resolve issues.
- Be the person who asks how their work is going and offers suggestions to become more productive.
- Adopt a policy of complete honesty.
- Be the boss who, if you don't understand exactly what an employee does, takes the time to find out.
- Thank people and congratulate them on a job well done.
- Delegate praise throughout the organization rather than taking credit for other people's work.
- Be the supervisor who values and encourages employees and their efforts.

Servant Leaders

Scrum says that the best leaders are "servant" leaders. These leaders center the people doing the work and find ways to assist them in becoming more successful. If you can meld the servant leader concept with Sahin's LMX theory, there's much greater employee buy-in, higher morale, and extremely productive teams with little turnover—precisely what most businesses want. This will truly make a difference in an organization.

Great Thinkers' Thoughts

Here is some great advice I've picked up from the great thinkers of our time on how to be the best leader.

Jim Collins. This former Stanford business professor, states, "Get the right people on the bus and the decision of where to drive the bus is the winner." First, get the right people. The "who" is ahead of strategy, ideas—ahead of *everything* else. If you have the right people, they already are motivated and disciplined. Another issue here is that the direction you're going is not important, because if you have the right people, you'll find your way in the best route.

Michael E. Gerber. This famed business advisor describes how to harness passion, vision, and intensity in business. A good speaker is someone who *wants* to speak and has the intensity to succeed. He's so motivated to speak that he truly becomes great at it. It's thinking positive that does the trick. As a boss, never tell people what they can't do because they will believe you. Tell people about their strengths and reinforce their good qualities.

This is great advice. If you want to hire a great leader, find someone so passionate about leading people and accomplishing your objectives that the person will be dedicated to meeting those objectives successfully. Imagine managing a team of people who are so completely fired up that all they want to do is accomplish your objectives! The issue? I'm not certain there is a huge supply of "ultra-motivated" individuals available for your team. You must discover how to transition people from a regular team into an extremely productive team. How can you accomplish this?

We've already seen an example of how to motivate people like this. Think about the bridge construction project described earlier in Chapter 3. The project manager provided financial incentives to his team whereby those team members knew they would be rewarded, potentially a lot of money, if they completed everything ahead of schedule. All the members of the project team became extremely motivated and pushed themselves and each other into a three-month early delivery. Therefore, it's not bullying them that makes them motivated, because that lowers morale and makes matters worse. No, it's providing incentives that does the trick.

Peter M. Senge. This famous MIT business lecturer maintains that leadership is how we create. Put spirit into the business, make people feel cared about, and people will become passionate about doing the work.

Certainly, Senge espouses the essence of Sahin's LMX theory. Make your people understand they are truly cared about. If you can take a team and make the members feel like they are family, the organization becomes their "home." They will do anything to fight for each other and accomplish great things together; they will feel emboldened to do their very best.

Marcus Buckingham. This British lecturer and business consultant states, "Never give negative feedback." Positive coaching will always make people better. Don't try to fix the bad parts; cultivate strengths instead. Excellence is about never fixing weaknesses but making the beautiful things even more beautiful.

John P. Kotter. This Harvard business professor devised an eight-stage process for change:

1. **Create urgency.** Kotter believes that 75 percent of an organization's management needs to buy in for a change to succeed. An open and honest discussion needs to take place. People have to feel the need for change. That need can create urgency, and the urgency will then begin to feed on itself.

   Reality? I think this concept is beyond critical! When I began working for a startup cellular company, we were all completely bought in and willing to do anything and everything to make it successful! It felt like it was just us against the world—an amazing beginning.

2. **Form a powerful coalition.** To lead change, you need to bring together a team of influential people within your

organization. This coalition works as a team, creates greater urgency, and builds momentum for the change. These people must be emotionally committed.

As long as the first point of complete buy-in is accomplished, then this is definitely the next step to bring the change to fruition. Nothing is worse than being all fired up and having no one to lead the charge.

3. **Create a vision for change.** A clear vision helps people understand why you're asking them to change. The vision should be easy to understand and remember.

   When I'm managing a major software implementation project, everyday workers become defensive because they resent the possibility that anyone might come in from outside the organization and tell them how to do things. This is not my style. I find it greatly satisfying to show these people respect, show them the vision, then ask them what would make their job easier. Most of these people have never been asked what would make their jobs better. They just are required to do as they're told. Over the years, many workers have given me marvelous ideas. At the end of the project, I make sure to give them credit. I don't say anything, generally, about the origins of these ideas until the end, because most managers believe low-level workers have stupid ideas. These managers have no inkling that their organization's greatest asset is the collective minds of their employees.

4. **Communicate the vision.** The success of your vision relies on effectively communicating that vision to the employees and getting their large-scale buy-in. A memo or special meeting is not enough. Talk about your vision constantly. Communication must go both ways. Listen to your people.

5. **Remove obstacles.** Once you have their buy-in, make it easy for your people to execute your vision. Remove barriers.

Obliterate obstacles. This takes diligence, listening, and patience combined with urgency. Transform "your" vision into "our" vision.

6. **Create short-term wins.** Success breeds more success, because success is motivating. Start with low-hanging fruit. Don't give critics and naysayers an opening to hurt your process.

7. **Don't declare victory too early.** Real change runs deep. Build on each success with a new goal. Analyze what went right and what needs to be improved.

   I like where he's going with this! My issue, however, is not to just look at the mission at hand for this. Rather, get everyone focused on being an entire organization looking for constant reinvention. When an entire organization gets fired up about constant improvement, you have an organization that will flourish!

8. **Anchor the changes in corporate culture.** For change to stick, it must become part of the organization's core. The values behind your vision need to become part of the culture. Both the company's leadership and the day-to-day work habits must continue to support the change.

Summing It Up

Perhaps the late Steve Jobs, who headed Apple, described the best management style around. He said, "It doesn't make sense to hire smart people and tell them what to do; we hire smart people so they can tell us what to do."

The servant leader perspective of scrum agrees with Jobs: a leader's role is to clear the path so the team can be successful. Leadership is all about empowerment. Those who can empower are the true leaders.

Of course, leadership can also go haywire, which I've seen in person.

Theory X

Over several decades of working mostly as an outside consultant, I've learned a lot about leadership styles. Unfortunately, there are evil, obnoxious styles that can destroy the fabric of an organization.

One of my worst experiences was with one of the large Theory X organizations, with each leader hired in the mold of the CEO (you may remember my description in Chapter 1). The CEO would literally get in front of someone who displeased him and scream profanities directly into the person's face, sometimes in front of hundreds of employees. His subordinates did likewise, making the organization sick with distrust and rampant turnover. The company asked me to fire 47 people shortly before Christmas, so it wouldn't have to pay year-end bonuses. My last day there was a celebration, and I no longer work for Theory X organizations.

A job interviewer once asked me, "How do you propose to get all the worthless employees off their asses and actually do something?"

I responded, "You value, listen to, empower, and treat them as part of the solution instead of being the problem." It was clear that this opportunity would not be a good fit.

The Best People Don't Work Here

I am always amazed when organizations bring in an outsider like me to lead major efforts while their company has multiple people qualified for that role. At a large hospital chain, I was tasked with managing the selection and implementation of complete financial and clinical systems for all their facilities. At the time, I was in my twenties. I discovered the reasons the company hired me.

- It truly believed that its people were working to their highest level of competence and that nobody was capable of doing better. The company always believed that someone from the outside was more qualified to do the work. Confidence soared when it brought in an expert, and that confidence helped projects succeed. Choosing one of its own would also have given that person a higher spot in the pecking order. Organizations are leery of promoting someone internally, knowing that they would have no place for this person after the project ended. Plus, if the project went sour, they couldn't blame one of their own without letting that person go.

- As an outsider brought in to salvage a project, I had instant credibility. The best people always wanted to work on my projects. This increased the likelihood of success and made my work life very pleasant.

- My expertise in business process reengineering has meant that organizations see me as much more successful than my competitors. Some of my best ideas were mine—but most were from the people who actually did the work. These employees held the secrets of understanding how to completely reorganize their companies. Their employers rarely listened to them, but I did. It was fun to credit the ideas' sources in my final report to executives. I hope the praise helped those employees rise in their professions.

Use Acting Skills to Get What You Want

I use my skills as an actor through all phases of business and life. I even taught a course at a local college called "How to Use the Skills of Acting to Get What You Want in Business and Life." In the rest of this chapter, I hope to get you interested in acting. Maybe it will add a new wrinkle in the way you work.

Many behavior and communication studies conclude that effective verbal communication can be broken down as shown in Figure 8.1. As you can see, 55 percent of all communication comes from body language and 38 percent from vocal tone, volume, pacing, and pitch. That leaves just 7 percent of meaning delivered by the words themselves.

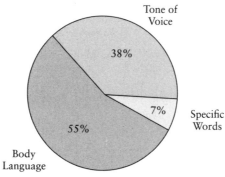

FIGURE 8.1 Effectiveness of communication.

It's your job to focus your team on accomplishing what you want it to accomplish. Sometimes there's a disconnect, even when you've worked hard to select every word you say. The misunderstanding might happen because your body language or tone of voice didn't agree with your words.

People pay close attention to the way you say something. You focus on the same informational cues from other people, too, whether you are aware of it or not. Have you ever watched someone talk and suddenly feel deep disbelief regarding what that person was saying? Have you suddenly developed a liking or dislike for someone when that person began talking? You were probably reacting to subliminal clues. If you could control giving out those subliminal messages, you would be a more effective leader.

Here is where acting comes in. The best actors make sure their body language and the pitch, tone, and volume of their voices match the specific words they speak. This makes them believable. Even without listening to the words, you would understand what the person means.

Here's a high-profile example of someone whose words and nonverbal communication didn't match. Mitt Romney, a moderate Republican in the 2012 US presidential election, knew he needed to come across as an archconservative to win his party's vote. He planned his speeches and debate responses—but he didn't believe what he was saying. A lifelong moderate cannot become a firebrand conservative overnight. In every speech or debate, poor Romney's body contradicted him from the beginning to the end. It's as though his body were saying, "I do not believe what I just said."

His opponent, Barack Obama, either believed what he said or was a wonderful actor. His body language, tone of voice, and pitch consistently matched the specific words he spoke. This made him believable. People who were looking for someone to believe in gravitated to him.

When you prepare to address other leaders in your organization, you should behave like an actor, putting thought into both what you'll say and how you'll say it. Try following these steps:

- **Step 1.** Like an actor, study all aspects of a character to determine the character's motivation in every scene. What is the character trying to accomplish? Why?
- **Step 2.** Decide what tactics you'll use to accomplish your goal.
- **Step 3.** Practice becoming the character.
- **Step 4.** Then practice in front of a mirror. Make certain your mannerisms, body language, and speech pattern fit the situation and accomplish what you intend.

- **Step 5.** Finally, practice in front of another person, take criticism, and try again.

Incorporate acting into your business approach, and you'll be better understood. You can test whether the people in your audience understand you. Ask them what they heard. If they didn't get what you tried to say, repeat it a little differently.

You can also see how your message lands by watching your audience:

1. Look for crossed arms. Perhaps the best action you can take here is to, in the middle of the talk, ask that person with crossed arms for her opinion. It's unorthodox, but it might help you discover something now that avoids a problem later.
2. Check to see if all eyes are focused on you. If someone's eyes are not on you, that person is not paying attention. Again, ask for that person's opinion.
3. Periodically pause the meeting and ask the audience to repeat the key points so far.

We can sum it up this way: just as the attendees are watching your body language and using it for understanding, you should be watching theirs for the same purpose. You can learn a lot.

CHAPTER NINE

Quality

Quality Is Different
Than Most People Think

Quality in terms of a project is a completely misunderstood subject. The level of quality refers to the degree of success the project had in meeting its objectives on time and at budget, not necessarily whether the product was produced at the highest quality. If, for example, your organization is creating a product at the low end of the market and the product is the cheapest in price and comparatively poorly made, the project can still be high quality. If the product fits the project objective, then it's a quality project.

Project managers should put real effort into determining what standards a finished project needs to meet and to what tolerance. Consider the common washer, the kind that fits over a bolt or screw and lets you tighten it until there is a snug fit. An imperfectly fit washer, the type known as an O-ring, caused the *Challenger* spacecraft disaster, which killed everyone on board. Some washers need very exact measurements. Other washers, which aren't used on spacecraft, don't need quite such mission-critical quality control.

Airplane bolts are another example. If the bolt is too short, the fuselage might be damaged during flight. If it's too long, cracks will form in the fuselage over time. Those bolts must be a precise length.

Think about the high level of accuracy needed in tools used for microsurgery. They must be extremely close to perfect. But if my new kitchen cabinets are not perfectly level when they arrive at my house, the contractor will add a shim or two and call that good enough.

Quality is defined very well by PMBOK (the Product Management Body of Knowledge). The only issue here is that it doesn't provide the reason for choosing one tool over another.

PMBOK defines confidence intervals. However, you are not told that a quality level of one standard deviation from the mean (68.27 percent confidence level) is conducive to a control chart. If you need an extreme, six sigma quality level, that takes many measurements, which, therefore, requires a scatter diagram.

Each industry has its own set of quality requirements. Manufacturing and construction have legal requirements that put them in a league of their own. I don't need to decide what quality of work is acceptable. Laws and industry regulations do that for me.

Software development is a different matter. With software development, every company should have development standards that enforce a certain level of quality. Integration testing, which checks that changes won't make other features fail, is the most important quality testing. This isn't defined as quality testing at all (nor is quality acceptance testing, which is not really testing). It's called scope validation, which ensures that the product is built to a standard that's acceptable to the customer.

Defining the Expected Quality Level

Quality in project management is defined by the requirements you gather from stakeholders. As they give requirements, you should be constantly asking them about the quality levels they need. They will generally give the right answer when they are asked the right questions in the best way. Simply continue asking to what level of quality must the job be accomplished to be acceptable? Do this, and you can avoid many problems by having to wait until acceptance testing to discover you missed a quality requirement and need to rework.

Quality is also defined in the project charter, where it asks for the measurable project approval guidelines. This is where the sponsor should spell out precisely what standards are necessary for the organization to accept the project, and this is when it is documented by the project manager. The agreement to this document is what authorizes the project to be performed.

In the beginning of my career, I managed a few large software development projects. When we presented our UAT (user acceptance testing) results, which proved that the project met the requirements specified in the project charter in the measurable project approval guidelines, the person I was dealing with told me that the company did not want what we had provided. I showed that person the project charter and was met with, "Well, that's obviously what I said because I signed it, but that's not what I want."

When You Met the Defined Quality but the Company Isn't Happy with the Result, What Do You Do?

First, you get the company to write a change request. You will have to determine how to fix the problem, and you cannot determine what to do or what your new plan will need without responding to a change request.

Then complete your investigation of the impact the change will have on the project's schedule, budget, and skill sets. Hope to get sign-off. If you can't, the situation may become a tad sticky.

After having had this happen to me a few times at the beginning of my career, I've concluded that the fix is to integrate scope verification as a normal process that's done repeatedly.

Scope verification means periodically taking what you have done so far to the customer and saying: "This is what we have so far. Are we on the right track? Is this acceptable to you?"

Through repeating this process often, you should be able to discover problems early enough to make changes, or hear that you've correctly interpreted the client's desires. There is nothing worse than completing a project and hearing that the client doesn't want the deliverable.

Different schools of thought define this practice differently. PMI defines the topic in its scope section, because user acceptance testing is a quality issue. Others refer to it as a quality control issue. Who cares? No matter what you call it, frequently showing a client your work to date can help eliminate the likelihood that the product will be rejected when it is complete.

I've heard software developers say: "We don't need to consider quality. We're professionals. We don't make mistakes." This is non-sense, of course. Software developers are as human and fallible as anyone else. The quality standards they use depend on the organization. Many organizations never define it, and that's the real problem. If it's never defined, how can it be achieved?

At a bare minimum, I usually require a significant effort at UAT to ensure that every feature works according to specification. Then we enforce a maintenance agreement that specifies the percentage of time the system is up and operational, as opposed to offline and unavailable.

Do Something About It!

I became sick and tired of shoddy coding techniques. In every situation where I've managed developers, I've required that we create development standards, if the organizations didn't already have them. Realistically, most organizations don't. When this is the case, one of our quality tests is always for conformity to development standards. Here are some of the reasons for having standards even though each of them will make the program less efficient, less sustainable, or more difficult to support the code. Again, these are just a small sample.

- Many database developers do not design databases for speed and durability. Are there orphan files, meaning files with no tie to other information from using a primary or other key? Are there alpha characters in the primary key? Alpha characters are frequently used in primary keys but shouldn't be. They force lookups, so the computer can understand what that letter is referring to. This always slows throughput.
- Does J2EE or .net development include loops like old C++ code?
- Is there inline code documentation, and if so, where and how?

Quality efforts should all be defined and estimated in the work breakdown structure. Never forget that testing must always be performed, so it must always be part of any estimate in work packages and activities.

CHAPTER TEN

Miscellaneous Notes

Do You Understand
Enough About Risk?

We made major changes to risk in Chapter 3 as we introduced topics such as how to determine a budget for risk, calculate expected time value, and how to earn value on risk. There are other places where managers should modify risk.

You could examine resource histograms, not just to determine if your team has all the skills at high enough levels to accomplish the task, but also to determine areas where essential people, especially area experts, may put the project at risk if they become unavailable for some reason. You must understand that if a particular team member is critical to your project's success, that person will likely be highly sought after, and you will likely have to evaluate alternatives as the project proceeds. Plans should include:

1. Training current staff to increase skill levels in those vulnerable areas.

2. Identifying, both internally and externally to the organization, other people with the necessary skills. Where unique knowledge is in the hands of only one or two people, insist that they thoroughly document the work they do. Include money and time for this in budgets and schedules, respectively. If necessary, build this documentation time directly into the WBS (work breakdown structure) and through the schedule development.

Another area where you need to be preemptive relates to quality standards. Decide what will happen when quality standards are not met. For example, materials might be of unacceptable quality, coding might not work as planned, or a new polymer might not pass stress tests. Plan for the time and money you may need for multiple tries at getting it right. Search the WBS for everything that could go wrong.

Plan to write contracts to avoid the risk of being overcharged, and manage the risk that the vendor could become financially incapable of finishing the project. What about your procurements?

You should determine the monetary and time impacts of every risk and include these in your plans. Moreover, you should think about work-arounds before you need them.

One of the best release managers I ever knew, Deborah Nicholas of Kaiser Permanente, was called the Queen of Plan B. When something didn't work at the last minute, she pulled out a Plan B that she'd already considered and had ready to go. She might have had four or five alternatives in mind—not just Plan B, but also plans C, D, E, and F. She was incredible and saved organizations a lot of money. I try to follow her example.

CHAPTER ELEVEN

Software of a Project Manager's Dream!

I understand that no software product currently available includes any of the features defined in this book or lets the user correctly perform all aspects of project management and strategic planning. Strategic planning software is a tool both for developing helpful ways of looking at SWOT and for facilitating creative thinking sessions.

Figures 11.1 and 11.2 show outputs designed in Ultimate PM. This is the software I've described earlier and shown output from. At the current time, UltiMentors is using it as proprietary for our customers. Sometime later, we'll make it commercially available.

To keep costs at a minimum while not reinventing all the wheels involved in basic project management products, I discovered an excellent, nearly complete shareware package that has tens of thousands of users and has been in existence more than ten years. Its user interface wasn't exciting, so we redesigned it with a modern look. It facilitates everything I recommend in this book.

As you begin, you can design a project either as a stand-alone or as part of a portfolio of projects supporting a strategic objective

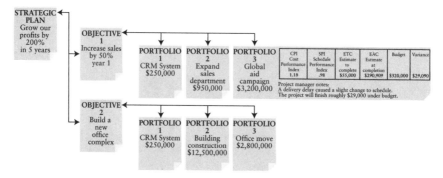

FIGURE 11.1 Strategic performance monitoring.

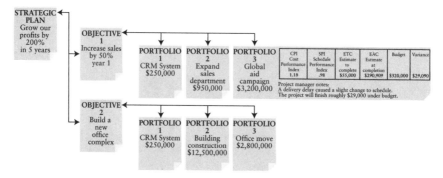

FIGURE 11.2 Using system-developed metrics, a detailed reporting of performance data to the level of activity is immediately available to stakeholders.

from your strategic plan. The advantage of selecting the portfolio is that one can dive deeply into how the strategic plan is performing as the project rolls up to strategic objectives, which in turn roll up to strategic plans.

When the project is first being considered, the project manager completes the project charter and then the project closure form, risk register, stakeholder register, and requirements traceability matrix.

The project manager and the preliminary team then begin to track their expenses through the project, so the initiating and planning expenses are automatically included in the budget.

Though the project is defined one milestone at a time, the software develops the WBS (work breakdown structure) automatically. Through a process of determining each work package's predecessor, the product autogenerates a network diagram that also can flow into the Gantt chart. The system automatically calculates slack from the network diagram, so slack items can be moved forward or backward for scheduling.

As the software estimates the WBS workload, it simultaneously creates a budget that automatically considers capacity planning and walks the project manager through risk identification and qualitative and quantitative risk analysis. The software steps you through questions so it can calculate the time value of risk as defined in this book.

The human resources section takes the project manager through the resource histograms to ensure the manager understands and uses the right skill sets. It asks for and adds the costs of hiring and/or training.

I'd love to add an extra feature to the human resources section: an organization-wide skills matrix that identifies and tracks all the skills an organization identifies for every resource in an organization. When your project identifies a skill set requirement for a PL/SQL architect (for instance), wouldn't it be nice to do a cross-organization skill set search and perhaps find one internally?

Another feature is a human resources section that can store project manager evaluations for each team member. Those evaluations can help future project managers get an objective view of team members' skills.

The quality section walks managers through planning all the tests and predetermining the required confidence interval for each test. The product adds these steps into the WBS, so managers can be influenced by capacity planning. As managers deal with fluctuations in measurement size during the actual tests, the system automatically modifies the sample size for achieving and maintaining the confidence interval.

The product design does not consider procurements, except to track the contract and expenses that are posted to the contract. It does add work packages, and so on, to the budget when these are necessary to manage the contract.

We described how the software works with integrated change control earlier.

Users can indicate when they are building the WBS that the project will be managed as agile. The system will build the budget appropriately if you plan the project correctly. Users can track the project budget and schedule and push selected code into production in two- to eight-week increments. I advise longer increments. Otherwise it's too much work to determine the percentage of completion that will kick off the next sprint. In the future, the system may integrate with a scrum software-tracking project such as JIRA or Confluence.

This product's best feature? It develops budgets and schedules accurately and reliably. It also tracks all expenses and costs, as well as each work package's completion, assigning earned value correctly. When managers identify new risks, the system uses risk response planning to assign positive or negative earned value. This is visible on status reports.

The product automatically generates status reports by rolling up portfolios of projects, which in turn roll up to strategic objectives and to the strategic plan itself. These are all visually represented with the output shown in Chapter 3.

Status reports are fluid and available as dashboards, which are constantly updated as the system applies expenses (which increases actual cost), marks work as completed, performs quantitative risk analysis, and generates earned value. Up-to-date status reports correctly identify how projects are performing at any point in time.

This is a web application that includes flexible dashboards. These dashboards let corporations, governments, taxpayers, banks, and other audiences see how projects are performing in real time—a handy feature when you want to monitor multiple projects, watch your tax dollars at work, explain yourself to voters, or decide whether or not to lend money to a government or corporation to fund a particular project.

CHAPTER TWELVE

Launching Pad

The name of this book, *Transforming Project Management: An Essential Paradigm for Turning Your Strategic Planning into Action*, easily conveys the purpose of this book. Strategic planning is more successful when you avoid the pitfalls that beset most organizations.

It's critical for organizations to understand precisely how much a project will cost, as a means of improving decision making. The processes I've defined will also vastly improve project management, especially through monitoring that lets the organization understand, at any point, exactly how the project is performing and, by rolling up the information, how the entire strategic plan is performing. The rolling-up process also enables high-level, real-time oversight.

As hinted at before, a software product that encapsulates every part of strategic planning and project management and that features all aspects of the budgeting and monitoring processes has been designed and is legally protected. This product is currently in use by UltiMentors. Our intention is to keep it completely proprietary and not sell it commercially. What we will do, instead, is use it as a tool for UltiMentors' professional services.

As mentioned, our markets are banks and politicians. The reason is simple. Bankers loan much money on projects with completely inadequate budgets. A typical situation may be a bank that loaned $25 million for a major project. The customer returns six months later saying, "We spent all the money and are only about 30 percent complete." Now the bank must decide whether it continues loaning more money until the project is complete (risking throwing good money after bad) or pulls the plug and writes off the loss.

For an UltiMentors' customer, the story would be far different. The bank would ask a business wanting a major loan to bring us in for, potentially, a more hearty yes or reduced interest rates based upon the lower risk. At that point, we would use our software product to determine a much more realistic budget, and then, after approval, we would use our product to produce weekly reports like the one shown in Figure 12.1.

Budget	Cost Performance Index	Estimate at Completion	Variance	Estimate to Complete	% Budget Spent	% Complete
$6,198,100.00	0.79	$7,860,842.81	−$1,622,742.81	$5,375,716.81	40.09	31.61

FIGURE 12.1 Implement CRM.

Armed with the information we provided, the bank can tell when a project is experiencing problems before that project becomes a disaster. In the example shown in the figure (taken directly from our software), the bank can see that, at the current pace, the project will be $1.7 million over budget. It also can see that over 40 percent of the budget has been spent but only 31 percent of the work has been completed. Now, at least, the bank has the opportunity to modify plans.

In the political realm, politicians using UltiMentors can establish a reasonable budget for a project like Affordable Care Act, the implementation of which was a disaster, and know they are doing a good job of managing taxpayer money. I recommend government organizations post these dashboards on a website so taxpayers can see how well their money is being managed.

Also, political parties may take advantage of politicians approving and managing projects that are failing by showing a plan to resolve the failures should these politicians be elected.

Certification

The PMP and SBOK certifications are woefully inadequate. The standards that you must know to pass the exam cannot be used to build a successful project budget or schedule, and they give very little insight into how to work with strategic planning or agile. Yet examination participants can get credit for their experience even when they've never managed a project by themselves, as a qualification to take the exam that proves they're at the highest level in the industry.

There must be something better. This book is the basis for a certification examination with an 80 percent passing level that requires an understanding of strategic planning as well as everything else necessary to be a vastly superior project manager.

The Pinnacle Project Strategist Certification is now operational.

Instructor:
Duane Petersen
PMP, MBA, SMC, SFC,
SPOC, CompTIA Security+
CEO of UltiMentors

U*lti*Mentors
intelligent business strategy and systems

ultimentors.com | Tacoma, Washington | 866-306-4103
Author of: Stop Strategic Planning into the Abyss

Figure **12.2** Author of *Transforming Project Management.*

Index

Page numbers followed by *f* indicate figures.

About the Author

Duane Petersen began his career trained as an industrial engineer, then soon after earned his MBA. Industrial engineers were once called "efficiency experts" and the drive to constantly discover improved processes and efficiencies has, in many ways, defined his career. This caused a major hurdle as his career trajectory drove him to strategic planning and project management arenas defined much more by failure than success. Something had to give, and it did. Duane began utilizing a business and industrial engineering approach to traditional methods and has revolutionized the industries.

Over the years, Duane began fine-tuning his processes with a number of large government agencies and Fortune 500 companies. This expertise enabled him to consult with provincial governors and bankers in China explaining his unique take on solving the problems of those industries.

As you will see in this book, his processes will drive project management to unseen levels of success, which will also enable strategic planning success.

Duane is now the CEO of UltiMentors, an organization known for providing superior project managers and training for customers utilizing these practices.